The Second City

ALMANAC OF IMPROVISATION

The Second City®

NORTHWESTERN UNIVERSITY PRESS | EVANSTON, ILLINOIS

ALMANAC OF IMPROVISATION

ANNE LIBERA

Northwestern University Press
www.nupress.northwestern.edu

Printed in the United States
10 9 8 7 6 5 4

ISBN-13: 978-0-8101-1801-0
ISBN-10: 0-8101-1801-7

David Shepard quote from *Something Wonderful Right Away: An Oral History of The Second City and the Compass Players* by Jeffrey Sweet (New York: Limelight Editions, 1987). Pages 7–8 in paperback edition.

Sheldon Patinkin quote from chapter 2 courtesy of Sheldon, from Martin's memorial service.

Bernard Sahlins's essay from *Days and Nights at The Second City,* copyright © 2001 by Bernard Sahlins, by permission of Ivan R. Dee, Publisher.

Bernard Sahlins quotes from interview done for book with Kelly Leonard.

All other quotes are from The Second City fortieth-anniversary panels.

As sources for his almanac, Jonathan Pitts credits Alan Baranowski, Danny Breen, Lenny Bruce, Del Close, Don DePollo, Martin de Maat, Michael Gellman, Ed Greenberg, John Michalski, Anne Morgan, Jonathan Pitts, Jeremy Pollock, Rob Riley, Kim Rhodes, David Shepard, Viola Spolin, and Jeffrey Sweet.

LIBRARY OF CONGRESS CATALOGING-IN-PUBLICATION DATA

The Second City almanac of improvisation / Anne Libera.
    p. cm.
    Includes bibliographical references.
    ISBN 0-8101-1801-7 (alk. paper)
    1. Improvisation (Acting). I. Libera, Anne.
PN2071.I5S43 2004
    792.02'8—dc22   2004002573

∞The paper used in this publication meets the minimum requirements of the American National Standard for Information Sciences—Permanence of Paper for Printed Library Materials, ANSI Z39.48-1992.

COVER PHOTOGRAPHS

Front cover top and back cover: Marc Hickox and Doug Morency (courtesy of The Second City)

Front cover middle, left: Eugene Levy, Dan Aykroyd, Gilda Radner, Rosemary Radcliffe, and John Candy (courtesy of The Second City)

Front cover middle, right: Adam McKay, Jenna Jolovitz, Scott Allman, Scott Adsit, and Rachel Dratch (courtesy of Jennifer Girard)

Front cover bottom, left: Samantha Albert, Keegan-Michael Key, Peter Grosz, Nyima Funk, Jean Villepique, and Andy Cobb (courtesy of Michael Brosilow)

Front cover bottom, right: Del Close and Avery Schreiber (courtesy of The Second City)

TITLE PAGE PHOTOGRAPHS

Gilda Radner (courtesy of The Second City); Del Close and Avery Schreiber (courtesy of The Second City); John Candy (courtesy of The Second City); Peter Grosz, Nyima Funk, and Jean Villepique (courtesy of Michael Brosilow)

TEXT PHOTOGRAPHS (courtesy of The Second City, The Second City Toronto, Michael Brosilow, Roger Lewin/Jennifer Girard Studio)

page 2: Samantha Albert, Andy Cobb, T. J. Jagodowski, and Jack McBrayer; page 26: Marc Hickox and Doug Morency; page 58: Maribeth Monroe; page 84: Abby Sher, David Pompeii, and Martin Garcia; page 106: Molly Erdman and Craig Uhlir; page 136: Scott Allman, Scott Adsit, and Rachel Dratch; page 162: Jenny Hagel, Matt Craig, and Joe Canale

Book design by Karen Keeley

CONTENTS

FOREWORD

In 1974 when The Second City opened in Toronto I had the good fortune to have Joe Flaherty, Eugene Levy, Gilda Radner, John Candy, and Rosemary Radcliffe as my first cast. There was no organized improv training program. It was trial by fire eight shows a week. Sometimes the fire was bright and hot, sometimes a few embers were wasted on audience members who wondered why these people couldn't just stick to a script. For me, there wasn't even a question. Watching this cast—even on a bad night of improv—was to experience chaotic, undisciplined brilliance.

Bernie Sahlins, Joe Flaherty, Sheldon Patinkin, and Del Close directed the early shows and conducted the improvisation classes that were open to the entire Toronto theater community. Improvisation was new and adventurous, and classes were in such demand that after the Mainstage show finished, the late-night improv classes would begin. It could be past midnight and you might discover actors from Toronto's "legitimate" theaters trying a gibberish scene. Something was up.

Cast members taught. People like John Candy, Joe Flaherty, Catherine O'Hara, and Sheldon Patinkin were teachers and inspired a new generation of comedic actors. Mike Myers, members of the Kids in the Hall, Nia Vardalos, and Colin Mochrie were all students. Their influence has been felt throughout the Canadian and American comedy scene for many years.

Mike Myers is one of the film world's most successful writer/performers, scoring huge hits with both *Wayne's World* and the Austin Powers series; Nia Vardalos wrote and starred in the highest-grossing independent film in moviemaking history, *My Big Fat Greek Wedding.* Is it not possible that something they learned at Second City contributed in some meaningful way? (On the set, the scene isn't working. Don't worry, I'll just tap into my years of improv training and try something different!) Okay—maybe it's confidence, maybe raw talent, but I think a case can be made for being schooled in Second City–style improvisation.

By 1988, three years after my partner Len Stuart and I had acquired The Second City Chicago, training at The Second City was still a semi-casual experience, with veteran alumni teachers like Don DePollo and Michael Gellman holding a few sessions every year. The time had come for the expansion and development of The Second City Training Center. Founders Martin de Maat and Sheldon Patinkin, along with administrator Cheryl Sloane, helped organize an educational program that sparked the extraordinary growth of improvisation as both an artistic and commercially viable art form. Bonnie Hunt, Chris Farley, Tim Meadows, Rachel Dratch, Tina Fey, Sean P. Hayes, Halle Berry, and even Oprah Winfrey all took classes at The Second City Training Center.

I've heard it questioned why an art form built on "making it up as you go along" would need formal training. It's an easy answer: just take a look at the alumni list. From 1959 to the present day, Second City alumni make up the comedic backbone of North America's entertainment industry. Second City alumni are known for "breaking the rules." But to break the rules you have to know them inside and out. One also need only look at the influence of improvisation on contemporary filmmaking and television to see that this once niche art form has become an integral source for creativity: the films of Mike Leigh and Christopher Guest, the success of television shows such as *Whose Line Is It Anyway?*, *Curb Your Enthusiasm,* and *The Bonnie Hunt Show,* and even Broadway's first improvised evening of entertainment called *Lifegame.*

The Second City Training Centers are the critical creative foundation for a Second City organization that has grown from a single stage to theaters and training facilities in Chicago, Toronto, New York, Detroit, Los Angeles, and Las Vegas. Each operation employs some of the best improv teachers in the world. They provide the spark that ignites so much young talent to make creative fire of their own.

—*Andrew Alexander*

INTRODUCTION

When I first started working and taking classes at The Second City in the late eighties, one of the great pleasures of working at the theater was the smallness of the office space and the intimacy that created. The actors would stand behind the box-office stool and talk about the show or how rehearsals were going. Touring companies would sit at the front bar and go over notes with their director or even rehearse and block scenes in the lobby in front of the box-office window. Many of the bar staff seemed to have been hired shortly after The Second City was founded in 1959 and had seen every performance and every improvisation created since that time. The history and lore of the place were all around you. After the show, you would go to the current incarnation of the bar across the street and talk improv theory with a group that could include bartenders, actors, directors, stage managers, musicians, and dishwashers.

Later, when I began to teach and direct, that sense of oral tradition continued. If you needed to know how to play a certain performance game or wanted to teach your class a new exercise, you called up Don DePollo, who had an encyclopedia of games in his head. Certain famous archive scenes were not captured on video, and the scripts, like those of Shakespeare, contained no discernible stage directions, but you just needed to call Sheldon Patinkin or Bernie Sahlins to get a detailed account of the original blocking. If you caught Joyce Sloane at the right time, she would even act out all the parts for you. As teachers, we all recognized that Viola Spolin's *Improvisation for the Theater* was the bible, but if you were stuck for how to approach a workshop you would sit down and have a few scotches with Training Center artistic director Martin de Maat, and he would give you a crash course in the fundamentals of whatever level of improvisation you wanted to cover.

Like any institution that is around for the long haul, The Second City has grown and changed. The Training Center had approximately a hundred students when I began classes but now teaches more than three thousand students annually. Of course, groups still sit "across the street" and talk about improv, but we are slowly losing our legends and our founts of information. Don DePollo simply didn't show up for his Monday night class one evening in the fall of 1995, and despite numerous promises, he and I never did sit down and capture the list of performance games that he carried in his head. In the winter of 2001, Martin de Maat died, leaving behind him a sheaf of notes for a book he never got to write.

This almanac is an attempt to capture the information and wisdom about the art and practice of improvisation that we have used and developed during more than forty years of work at The Second City. It is not complete; no book on this work could be at this point, because improvisation as we practice it is a very new art form and innovations and discoveries are being made every day. My mission is simply to give you a taste of how many of us learned the theories of improvisation, one teacher and opinion at a time.

As you read, I'd like you to imagine yourself sitting at the front bar of The Second City Mainstage in Chicago. There is a blue-and-white paper cup of really awful overcooked coffee in front of you. The wall behind you is covered with black-and-white photographs—photos from shows, cast pictures. Many of those in the photos are familiar. Some are easy to name; others require you to check the label under the picture. Everyone has a lot more hair than they do now. Another wall contains a list of every person who has ever created a resident company show for Second City.

Think of each essay as someone sitting down next to you at one of the red-vinyl-covered stools that line the wooden bar and having a conversation with you about some aspect of improvisation. Frequently a contributor will contradict someone else and that's part of the process. In an art form based on agreement, probably the only thing we all agree on is that there are as many approaches to improvisation as there are practitioners. As we go along, I'll jump in to make introductions, clarify a concept, or help define terms. Everyone walks by the bar on the way to rehearsal or class, so we'll also have other directors, teachers, actors, alumni, and perhaps a former dishwasher or two share a comment or a story from their own experiences watching and performing improvisation. And like any really good conversation, there will be digressions and maybe an argument or two. But let's start where almost all conversations about improvisation begin—with Viola Spolin and the basics.

—*Anne Libera*

The Second City

ALMANAC OF IMPROVISATION

CHAPTER ONE: **BEGINNING**

Viola Spolin

The thread that's running through all this is Viola Spolin, whom I consider a genius. When we asked her about particular points [of improv games], she said: "I really don't know how that game goes, or any of them really. I was in a state of revelation when I wrote them." I believe that, because everything about the games informs Second City, it informs interpretive work. It's about the job that the actor has to do. It's about being present, about being in a play, about being in an ensemble because of that combined energy. I think that's why Second City is enduring and probably will endure. It has that fluidity. It's connected to the art.

—*Joyce Piven*

Paul Sills asked me to join his mother's workshop. She was then putting together a book on improvisation for the theater. Myself and Dick Schaal and Hamilton Camp—there were five of us—and [Del Close and John Brent]. We were a part of that group. We worked with her every day. It was a five-days-a-week thing. She always had food for us. I carry on that tradition in my workshop; I bring food so that when the actors get a little low on energy, they can have something to come back with. She fed us as well as nurtured us in other ways. The most important thing that she taught me was the necessity of being open and creative and true in everything you do. That's what I've tried to do.

When Paul asked me to attend workshops with his mother, Viola Spolin, I was excited. Imagine my surprise when, gathered together in a room at the Lincoln Hotel in Chicago, Viola asked me to describe what I had learned at the Goodman [School of Drama]. When I mentioned that conflict was basic to acting classes there, she told me that conflict was anathema to her workshops. I thought, Five years of training out the window. Well, not completely. I learned that all the other techniques I had been taught were applicable if I modified *conflict* with *agreement*. As Viola said, "You can't have conflict unless you agree to have conflict. The war is fought until one side doesn't agree to fight anymore. A new agreement has to be made. Agreement is basic to the health of creative improvisation. Conflict alone is static. It can't go anywhere."

Viola shook up many basic beliefs I had about my work as an actor. To ask me to keep my mind out of the work and allow the experience to come unencumbered was tantamount to asking me to turn off my lungs for an hour or more so that I could learn how to breathe better. It was clear that there were no shortcuts. The best way to get from point A to point B was in a totally illogical direction. While experiencing the elements of such a journey (surprise!), you got there. And it was fun. And it was an adventure. And this "path" worked. It was "The Method" of improvisational theater, as replete with multiple truths, insightful experiences, and discoveries of the soul and mind as any method of acting.

—*Avery Schreiber*

First Class

Joyce Piven and Avery Schreiber spoke about Viola Spolin at The Second City's fortieth-anniversary panel on the beginnings of Second City. Viola Spolin was the mother of original Second City director and cofounder Paul Sills and it is only appropriate that we begin with Viola. Almost everything we teach or practice at Second City can in some way be traced back to Viola, either through her seminal book Improvisation for the Theater *or through those she trained—many of whom, like Avery and Joyce, Del Close, and Martin de Maat, went on to become master teachers themselves.*

When I do new-student orientation for The Second City Training Center

I begin by saying "This work will change your life." It's hard to believe that when you take your first class, lulled by the seeming simplicity of the beginning Spolin exercises, but I'll let Frank McAnulty, who teaches a great many first classes for our program in Toronto, explain how it happened to him.

"Level 1"; "The Beginners"; "Level A"; "Introduction to Improv"... it has many names and I find it one of the most exciting parts of teaching improv at The Second City: the first class for the first time.

Let me tell you a little about what it was like for me my first time in Level 1. I started my career at The Second City completely by accident. I was working as a cameraman on *Wide World of Sports* (the Canadian version) and as assistant director on a TV series shot here in Canada called *Strange But True.* The producer at the time told me that I would get to direct some of the episodes in season two, but I would have to learn "actor speak"—the strange language that actors speak to each other. Phrases like, "What's my motivation?" Me, I could tell them what lenses we were using and how many pages we were shooting that day and what time "kraft services" would be set up . . . but all that "emotional needs" crap . . . I knew nothing.

I set off to find some acting classes. To my horror I found that you had to audition to get into these classes. . . . I was screwed! Then a buddy told me about The Second City improv classes: you pay, you're in. I was a winner. I went down to the Old Firehall—back in my day, the home to The Second City here in Toronto—paid my sixty dollars for six classes and I was in!

My first class was a mix of highly skilled, lightly skilled, and confused performers. I was a member of the latter group. I thought I could sit at the back of the class, take notes on "actor speak," and return to *Strange But True* to take my highly deserved spot behind the camera. Well, no such luck. I was told, "Here at The Second City we don't allow people to audit the classes." I feigned knowledge about what "audit the classes" meant and slowly—very slowly—it dawned on me: "Shit, I have to get involved, I have to do this!" I got up, joined the circle, and started pointing at people and saying their names. Hey—I can do this . . . I can . . . what? You want me to stand opposite somebody and mirror his movements? What the hell is that going to teach me? Hey—this isn't so bad after all. I hear laughter, giggling. . . . This is kind of fun! We're all doing the same stuff so nobody looks like an asshole. I think I could get used to this.

After my third class—a makeup class with Jeff Ellis, director of the National Touring Company at the time (information that I would not know until a little later)—I came home to a message that I should call The Second City and ask for Jeff. The jig was up; they knew I was just taking classes to further my personal agenda. I didn't belong in the world of improv. I felt sure I was getting the boot!

I phoned Jeff, prepared to fight my case and tell him I planned to stay in the classes and maybe even move on through all the levels—so there! Well, Jeff asked me if I wanted to audition for the National Touring Company. Oh no—the audition thing again! I timidly said yes and two days later I went to the audition with about two hundred other people. Hey, I got a callback. . . . That's good, right? Good if you don't plan to sleep that night, which I didn't. The next day there were eighteen of us, three groups of six. Some of us knew each other, some were strangers, and some were just strange. We went through about eight exercises, seven of which were explained to me by the very people I was competing against.

Jeff came out and asked three people to stay: Mike, Mike, and Frank. *Lucky assholes,* I thought to myself. . . . Hey wait, he said "Frank." I looked around. . . . Anybody else here called Frank? Why the hell is my classmate, the person who was my partner for most of the callback, Enio Mascherin, smacking me on the back and congratulating me? Frank? Me Frank? There's been a mistake. Me? I'm in? Well, kind of in—one of the "Mikes" and "Frank" are going to be understudies. The other "Mike," a fellow named Mike Myers, he got in—the real "in."

I was an understudy for just over a year and then I got "in." A year in which I took advantage of every free class I could get into, sometimes taking a class every day of the week. Thus began what to this day, seventeen years later, still with The Second City, I call ". . . the best job I ever hated or the worst job I ever loved."

I have taught at The Second City for about fourteen years now, at all levels—according to whatever they were called at the time: Level 1, Level A, Level 6, Level 6 plus, Performance Level, Script Class, Conservatory 1, Conservatory 1A. My favorite levels are for the most part the beginning levels, A through E, where you still have a mix of different people taking the classes. Some individuals want to be performers with The Second City, some want to start their own troupes, some just simply enjoy improv, and some are really good improvisers but have well-paying straight jobs and don't want to give up the security of the regular paycheck.

Level A is the first class. This is where the funniest person on the loading dock meets the funniest person in the office, who meets the funniest person in the parish, who meets the shy person trying to come out of her shell, who meets the Jim Carrey wannabe, who meets the person who just finished a toastmaster class and wants to learn to "wing it." This is my class and I love it.

Out of the hundreds of classes I have taught, I might have disliked three or four of them. I have had individuals that I've disliked but rarely a whole class, and I don't think ever a Level A Class. I love the nervous energy of Level A. I love that they are so willing to learn. I love the fact that they think I've got something to teach them. After every first Level A Class that I've taught, I thank the improv gods for sending me the most gifted individuals. Around the third or fourth class of Level A, I have a more educated opinion of the class.

I expect more out of my students, and they seem to enjoy that. From about the second class on, I frame all of the exercises in the Who, What, Where format. I figure that if it's scenes we want to eventually teach them, let's teach them in a scenic format from the beginning.

I use the Viola Spolin method—with one little difference. I reverse the information. Instead of asking them to set up a Who, What, Where and telling them that they will only be able to speak one word at a time, I ask them to set up a Who, What, Where . . . and then just before they start to perform the exercise I tell them, "Oh by the way, you can only speak one word at a time." I find this way it screws up any pre-planning they do and they end up keeping the three W's in a very simple and easy format.

I also allow them to be as blunt as they wish, as racist as they want, and as sexist as they want. I've found that when you allow people to do whatever they think will get them a laugh, they tend to find out quickly the audience doesn't agree with them. My experience has been that tasteless material is rooted out of an actor's performance quickly when it is greeted by silence.

I also give notes in a very blunt manner, or so I've been told. After a couple of classes the students seem to be used to it. I always try to find something positive in what they are doing but I want them to learn that what they are doing is disposable and that they shouldn't take it personally. If you have one bad scene and carry that baggage into the next scene, you're not existing for your partners—you're just trying to please "the fish" (the audience). When "the fish" know you're there to please them ... the job gets a lot harder.

Why do I call them "the fish"? The next time you're onstage and you've got them—"the fish"—watch them. They move forward to listen to you; they follow you from stage right to stage left like you're the only food source they've ever set eyes on. If you lose them, they lean back like a fat trucker pushing four pounds of undercooked steak away and grunting for the waiter. When the audience no longer feels like voyeurs looking in on a unique moment in a character's life, I think you've lost them. You're going to have to work your ass off to get them back.

In the first couple of levels, I try to teach the students to keep things as simple as they can. What makes a scene work is their commitment to it; what each cast member brings to it. Your thoughts on a subject are going to be different from mine even if we agree. As Del Close said to one of the casts I was in during rehearsals: "If it's not important to you, why should the audience care?" Or as Michael Gellman said a little more succinctly, "You know what this scene needs? A fucking opinion!"

With every class I teach I remind myself that most of these students are just like me when I started. They've never had an acting class; they don't know upstage, downstage, stage left, and stage right. They don't know about upstaging or projecting or articulating or staying in the moment. They don't know any of that and sometimes that is a good thing!

There are some rules I try to teach my students. Rules like the rhythm of comedy—that comedy generally works in threes, fives, or sevens. Improv scenes generally succeed when you have (1) abnormal people in normal situations or (2) normal people in abnormal situations. You have less success when you have abnormal people in abnormal situations (with the exception of Monty Python and The Young Ones, both of whom could make anything funny). You'll probably have little to no success when you have normal people in normal situations . . . because it's just way too boring. A big rule I cram down my students' throats is *"No questions!"* Questions are like asking for permission for your idea. Questions are like turning to the other actors and saying, "I have an idea. Why don't you come up with it?" A question is like a huge pause in the middle of an exchange while the other actors try to figure out what you want. Some students insist that questions are needed so that you can find out about the other person. I gently remind them about making assumptions about endowing the other person with information. I just love to watch restaurant scenes that start with, "Would you like to see a menu?"; "Yes please, could you tell me the specials?"; "Sure, what do you like?" At that point I'm on my feet screaming, "Great! Another slow start! In case you don't get it—this is another fucking restaurant scene!" Cut to the chase . . . please! Finally, after "gently" nurturing them through the teaching of all the rules of improv, I tell them one more thing: that all the rules are there for breaking . . . just find a great way to break them!

—*Frank McAnulty*

The Rules

When I first started taking classes at Second City, Martin de Maat clearly defined what he referred to as the "Big Three," the three most important rules of improvisation. They were, in what seemed to be ascending order of importance: Story, Questions, and Denial. Quite simply, a trio of don'ts —don't talk about the past or future. Don't ask questions. Don't say no. These don'ts were accepted as givens for good improvisation, and in fact, there were an entire series of exercises in which your instructor or fellow classmates would buzz you out of a scene if you committed any one of the three infractions.

While the simplicity of the Big Three is useful for teaching beginning improvisers, it is also problematic. For some improvisers the list of rules immediately puts them up in their heads. They slip into instant judgment of themselves the minute a question crosses their lips and they find it almost impossible to stay focused on the scene. It's also not that unusual to

"Yes, and . . ." and "Explore and Heighten"

The concepts of "Yes, and . . ." and "Explore and Heighten" are two slightly different approaches to the same essential idea. Every improvisational offer should be fully accepted and built upon.

The beauty of "Yes, and . . ." is its simplicity. In the classic improv exercise Ad Game, improvisers attempt to brainstorm a marketing campaign for an imaginary product. Every time someone new speaks she must begin her first sentence with "Yes, and . . . ," thus enthusiastically agreeing to and building upon the previous player's idea. By being forced to accept and enhance what their partner has provided, improvisers find themselves surrendering their own "better" ideas and instead creating a concept that could not have existed without the parti-cipation of the entire ensemble.

"Explore and Heighten," while not quite as easily accessible an idea as "Yes, and . . . ," has a somewhat wider application within scene work. We explore an activity, say washing dishes, by doing it in a variety of ways—scrubbing, rinsing, wiping. We involve our senses in the activity: seeing the bubbles, feeling the heat of the dishwater, smelling the soap. We heighten dishwashing by adding intensity: we wash faster or with larger and more extended movements. We also heighten by raising the stakes of the activity; perhaps the dishes are exceedingly valuable or we are being forced to wash them at gunpoint. Ideally, if something is fully explored and height-

find that if you are concentrating hard enough on not saying something, that very concentration causes you to instantly speak the words you meant to avoid.

Also, as Mick Napier has frequently pointed out (and proven in his work at the Annoyance Theater, where rules for improvising are actively eschewed), you can have a perfectly wonderful scene in which every one of those rules is repeatedly broken. Perhaps more troubling, you can also improvise an absolutely terrible scene while remaining completely within the boundaries of these improvisational dictums. And let's face it: we want our improvised scenes to mirror reality, to create recognizable human behavior on our stages. In real life people ask questions; they tell stories to each other. People say no to each other a million times a day in a thousand different ways.

However, if you take a close look at each of the rules, you can discover a basic underlying truth that exists in any good scene regardless of the number of times the rule proper may be broken. Once you are aware of this underlying truth it also becomes possible to shift your focus away from what not to do and on to ideas and concepts that are active and positive.

Let's begin with "Denial" or "Don't say no." The underlying principle here is that in order to improvise well we must agree that the improvisers onstage all exist within the same universe and that universe has consistent rules. Everything built or asserted by any member of the ensemble is valid and true *from their perspective.* Whatever choice our fellow improviser has made, we must support the fact that he made it and that it is true for his character. Characters may be wrong, be misguided, or have opposing wants or goals but the improvisers always remain in agreement on the basic truth within the scene.

That's pretty heady theory and not necessarily easy for a beginning improviser (or any improviser, for that matter) to use while in the moment onstage. Improvisers tend to use denial when they are in judgment of the quality of the scene, their partners, or their own choices. So, instead of focusing on denial, we try to practice supporting our partner. We surrender our own idea of where the scene might go, and to quote Viola Spolin, we "follow the follower." We use the principle of "Yes, and . . . ," not only agreeing that each new offer is true and valid but also building on every offer made rather than spinning off in a new direction. We explore and heighten each new moment until the moment transforms and presents us with something new to explore and heighten.

"Questions" tend to shift responsibility for the scene heavily onto one player. In an improvised scene they are often filler; they take up time without providing any information. The underlying truth behind the "no questions" rule is that each player must take responsibility for their part in building the scene.

We use questions to avoid taking focus. Students who have trouble in this arena practice give-and-take focus, forcing themselves to fully take focus when it is given to them. We ground ourselves in an environment, using objects to give that environment depth and reality. We try to make discoveries in the scene so that everything we need to know is right in front of us without our needing to ask for it.

"Story" has always been the most complicated and misunderstood of the dialogue rules. We are told, "Stay out of story" and "Don't talk about the past or the future." For me, the underlying principle here is in many ways clearer and easier to follow than the original rule: "Everything each character does or says should affect the other characters onstage."

Just like denial and questions, going into story comes from fear and judgment of ourselves and our partners. It is easy to chatter about what we might do because we are afraid that doing it would result in a boring scene (thus ironically we create a boring scene filled with chatter). To move ourselves away from the concept of story, we instead focus on the relationship between the two people onstage. We participate in an activity that allows us to demonstrate our characters' reactions through behavior. We raise the stakes of the current moment until our characters cannot help but be propelled to action. We find a game in the scene with our partners, keeping ourselves in the present moment. We maintain awareness of our own and our partner's status; we change status as a way of demonstrating how each action affects our character.

Of course, no one can hold all this in their head and speak at the same time. We learn to improvise just as we learn to drive a car; at the start our brains are full of details and instructions and then eventually we stop having to remind ourselves to watch the mirrors or check our distance from the nearest car; it becomes second nature. Ironically, for the improviser that is the point when the Big Three seem to become valuable again. For

ened, a change will happen organically —a transformation will occur. In our dishwashing example, the heightened speed or intensity could cause a dish to fall and break, creating a new activity—cleaning up—which can itself be explored and heightened. Improvisers who learn how to explore and heighten each beat or moment within a scene find that they can simply ride the events of the scene as a surfer rides a wave, without needing to work at making anything special happen.

teachers and directors the rules function as red flags—signals that performers are afraid or uncomfortable. Any experienced performer who finds he is consistently breaking the rules knows that he should check to make certain that his focus and priorities are in order. Most scenes are better if you say yes, make statements, and stay in the present. In fact, Mary Scruggs, who heads our Writing Program, begins her rewriting workshops by having her students remove all Story, Questions, and Denial from their written sketches. The scenes immediately improve, providing an object lesson of what made us study the rules in the first place.

I'm trying to avoid some painful pun here along the lines of "Speaking of object lessons. . . ." Still, if there is anyone who would appreciate the unavoidable pun it would be Tim Kazurinsky. Tim appeared on The Second City Chicago Mainstage in the late seventies before going on to perform on Saturday Night Live *as well as write and act in numerous films. When I first started working at Second City there were pictures up in the box office from Tim's wedding with the entire bridal party in Groucho glasses.*

Object Work, or "A Mime Is *Not* a Terrible Thing to Waste"

To improvise, you need a bare stage, actors, and chairs.

Everything else is pretend.

Everything:

The putter.

The golf ball.

The spatula.

The pancake in the air, midflip.

The plunger.

The toilet you're jamming it into.

The blueprint of the bank you're gonna knock over.

The not-yet-dead fish on the line.

The stinky French cheese on your plate.

The large painting of your dinner host's naked wife.

The brain you are transplanting.

And the ever-popular proctoscope hose.

The trick is to pretend that none of this is pretend.

The other trick is to remember where you put these things.

If you create a dining-room table early in the scene, you can't just walk through the damn thing later on in the scene.

ILLUSTRATION 1

When you set your drink down somewhere, you better remember where. Because the audience will. They'll also remember if you were drinking from a rocks glass, a stein, a champagne flute, or a brandy snifter. Each has a peculiar shape and must be held in a particular fashion.

As you create a scene, you fill it with assorted pieces of furniture and various items. Your observance of the physical properties of these things—and the manner in which you manipulate them—is called *object work*.

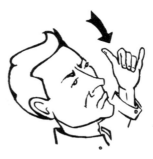

ILLUSTRATION 2

The audience should never be aware of your object work. It should be so natural as to become invisible. If the audience does notice your object work, you will be labeled a "mime" and be taken out back and flogged. Because, despite what your high school drama teacher told you, nobody likes mimes.

Quite often, if a scene is in trouble, an actor will make a phone call. Look now, if you will, at the accompanying illustrations.

Illustration 1 demonstrates the correct way to hold a phone. Illustration 2 demonstrates a pathetic attempt by some idiot to transform his hand into an actual handset. (I smell a flogging.)

If a scene is totally tanking, someone invariably whips out a gun.

ILLUSTRATION 3

Illustration 3 demonstrates the correct way to hold a gun. Illustration 4 demonstrates that the actor clings to an infantile belief in animism and should be doing children's theater.

Object work. Keep it simple. Keep it real. Or the rest of the cast will be calling you "Marcel" behind your back.

—*Tim Kazurinsky*

Environment

The title of Tim's essay is a reference to an old Second City habit of giving shows two titles connected by an or—*both titles are generally puns; a recent example would be the ETC show* Holy War, Batman! or The Yellow Cab of Courage. *My own personal favorite "or" title was never used—*The Wreck of the Edmund Serves Coffee. *It's an in-joke. Edmund is a tall, thin, pale man*

ILLUSTRATION 4

with the voice of Lurch from the Addams Family. He comes to Second City every Saturday night and makes cappuccino and espresso for the staff and performers. I don't know the origins of this or when it began, although Edmund was certainly already well established when I began working in the box office in the mideighties. The sight of Edmund's antiquated equipment and the smell of slightly burned coffee immediately takes me back to a specific place and time in my own life. It's a reminder of one of the other benefits to the improviser of object and environment work—specific objects and sensations can ground you and create an emotional state, a strong starting place from which to begin a scene.

The more objects you discover in a space, the more detailed it becomes, the accrual of those objects along with sensory information becomes an imaginary theater set or a real-life space, what Viola Spolin called the Where. This is as true for the most advanced performer as it is for a beginning student. Bruce Hunter teaches all of these levels and is one of our most popular teachers at our theater in Toronto, where he also performed in the early eighties.

Teaching environment for me is a way to stop the students from thinking about stuff that is going on somewhere else, like another galaxy or even another level of consciousness. Not that this particular work isn't worthy but it seems more productive to concentrate on a point before we start pondering the universe.

In all the beginning classes, I have noticed that people have difficulty when I introduce "environment." The initial reaction is, "I can't do mime." But it's not mime that we work on; the real skill developed by getting actors to focus on and think about the world around them is exploration. Suddenly the actor is in a reality that he or she must share with the other actors; communication through the objects and the environment is essential. Introduce the environment and the actor must become a better observer. People often laugh at how much emphasis I put on environment, but I challenge anyone to write a story that does not include some sort of environment. It is almost impossible. People communicate largely by what they do. When you notice another actor and his or her relationship to the environment it gives you ideas. If everyone in the scene has trouble with the can opener, not only does it become a bit, but it tells the audience what kind of people we are dealing with. Are these lazy individuals that never bother to get another can opener? Are they too poor to buy another can opener? Or are they just stupid and can't use a can opener? Is there one character that has no problem with the can opener? How do the others feel about him? Even with something so simple, we have added another layer to this glorious make-believe. Ignore the environment and we lose hundreds if not thousands of opportunities. Understanding the tools needed to create these stimuli allows the character to react honestly and takes the stress off the actor to come up with something off the top of his or her head.

Environment dictates action. It can also dictate inaction. Let me explain. In any given place there are activities that suit that environment. When you are in a washroom it is unlikely that you are swinging a golf club. Just seeing someone practicing his swing tells us he is at a golf course, but that does not mean one choice overrides another. An action that normally denotes an environment can be accepted and taken at face value. The golf course scene can move forward from this point and can be used as an example of accepting an offer. On the same hand, as soon as someone else enters and establishes a bathroom we have a conflict. It does not mean that the person entering is pimping the other actor and wasn't paying attention. It means that the second player has seen the action and is establishing an environment that will create conflict. I have also seen new students do this totally unaware, get a laugh, and make a note in their comedy brain on how to get a laugh at someone else's expense. They do not recognize that trust plays a big part in changing the direction of an offer. Hopefully they were working with someone who trusted their choices and didn't hate them for what might appear to be "blocking." But we will not discuss that now.

Not all choices have to be so crazy. Characters can be realized on so many different levels when the environment affects them. How does the pen feel? If the actor decides for himself that it is a heavy expensive fountain pen, that will change his character, his status, and his actions. A character will react differently when she is comfortably at home than she will if she is stuck on a crowded bus. Even knowing that some characters would not normally fit into a certain surrounding creates interesting choices. A bishop at a strip club. A policeman at a mafioso wedding. A car salesman in

ENVIRONMENT DESCRIPTION: One of my favorite environment exercises is an extension of the floor plan exercises detailed in Spolin. Players take turns describing the environment, building on each other's description. The teacher or director should side-coach players to be as specific as possible: "What shape is the couch? What is the color or texture of the couch's fabric? Are there cushions?" Players move around on the stage as they describe parts of the environment, showing the exact size and location of each element. Once the structure of the space has been created, other elements can be added—time of day and year, temperature, sources of light. The players then do a scene in this fully detailed environment, allowing their creation to influence the scene without making the environment the focus of the scene. In other words, they shouldn't talk about the environment, they should respond to it.

an Amish town. Without environment the characters stumble from one limbo to another. In all these cases environment allows the actors a chance to breathe. Once the actor recognizes his relationship to different environments a lot of choices are already made. Even just using the objects around you can cause conflict. You can't go to the bathroom if you inadvertently glued your hands to the desk. You can't tell the boss you think he is a moron if he is sitting there cleaning his handgun.

If you don't know where you are, how do *we* know where you are? Why would we care about your struggle when we can't see it in the context of your surroundings? If a scene starts to die, go to the environment. Take charge. Do something! Pick up a book, find a note, make some lunch, look for your watch, peel a grape. Something will happen. The environment will ground you. It gives you a place to come back to when what you are saying is of little interest.

I want to be clear that we should never replace the message or the direction of the material with simply jumping from one object to the next. It must be something that an improviser practices so that it becomes second nature—so that the actor can look around an empty space and see a palace. The environment and all the things in it can become a major key to consistent improvisation. It is comforting to know that when all the senses come together—what we see, what we hear, what we taste, what we smell, what we touch—a wonderful world of choices is opened up and is ready for the picking. So, have a grape and ponder space.

—*Bruce Hunter*

Give and Take

Viola Spolin's Rigid Give and Take is one of the first exercises taught in any beginning improv class, right after Mirror and some sort of Space Walk. It's not the most exciting of exercises—it's not scenic, it's not a game. It's probably the closest thing that improvisation has to playing scales on the piano.

I won't take the space here to detail the exercise in full because Sheldon Patinkin gives a very complete description in his chapter on using improvisation in acting, but the giving and taking of focus is such a fundamental element of improvisational work that it deserves its own space in this chapter on basics.

We practice giving and taking focus so that we can be in control of the audience's eye—we have no director to block the action, so the players themselves must be responsible for the picture on the stage, making certain that the audience sees and is aware of everything necessary to enjoy the performance. An ensemble with expertise in giving and taking focus is a pleasure to watch; there is a flow to the scene. The ball of focus passes smoothly from one player to the next. Our eye alights on a character and it seems as if magically he is doing something that furthers the scene. And no matter how clever or inventive the performers, if the focus is muddy the scene falls apart—players interrupt each other, interesting initiations are missed and dropped. The audience becomes confused and, not knowing what to pay attention to, stops paying attention altogether.

We take focus physically with movement, with sound, with energy, and with a heightened presence. We give focus with our attention, through listening, through eye contact, with gestures (pointing), and verbally (asking someone a question, calling on someone by name). To use the obvious metaphor we pass focus like a basketball, only there is no opposing team. As in a game, we remain alert, ready to take the focus when it is passed to us, aware of when we are open and when we are not.

The exercise Give and Take becomes the underlying structure of almost any scene or game we play. We give and take focus with ease, nearly unconsciously in a two-person scene. Within group scenes, scenes with entrances and exits, or games that require editing, an awareness of focus takes precedence over nearly everything else. Whichever player has focus is, by necessity, the one driving the scene at that particular point in time. It is possible to improvise a group scene as an extended and slightly more animated game of Give and Take. The players follow where the focus leads, adding to the scene when the focus lands on them. When this kind of scene is done well it is especially pleasing for an audience—on a certain level the audience feels that they are playing along with the actors, and the performers are following where the attention of the audience lands.

Because the audience doesn't know (or care) whether focus is taken intentionally or unintentionally we must even more strongly embrace our focus mistakes when we are improvising scenically. There are no accidents or mistakes in improvisation unless we make them so. If you trip and fall, claim the accidental focus and make use of it; add to the scene. Fall into the crack in the game, as Second City performer and teacher Rick Thomas used to say. Similarly, if you are in the back line of a long form piece that requires editing, be aware that once you have made a move to edit, there is no going back. Simply by making the move you have pulled focus away from the scene in progress. The audience is watching you now; make the most of it and forge ahead. And please don't be the guy who is constantly moving while in the back line, the one who pulls focus from the scene onstage with his exaggerated responses to the action and telegraphs his intentions to edit a full minute or more before he actually does so.

The following exercises use the skills of giving and taking focus:

Unconducted Story. Players take turns telling a story as in the classic conducted game but each takes focus in order to continue the story. Practice this first in a circle with eye contact and then in a line.

Restaurant. Two or more couples are at tables in a restaurant. Give and take focus between tables.

Entrances and Exits. Each time a player enters a group scene, he must strongly take focus and all players who are already onstage must give it. Each time someone exits she must take focus for a moment and give it to someone onstage as she exits. In the performance version of this game, each person is given a word (a type of fruit, a color, a mode of transportation), and depending on whether he is on- or offstage, he must enter or exit if his word is said within the scene.

Also, the Hypertext game described in chapter 3 is good practice in what Spolin calls "No Motion"—that is, being engaged in the scene while still not taking focus from what is primary.

Where We Came From: A Very Brief History of Revue

Before we leave the topic of beginnings, I want to add a little historical perspective courtesy of Bernard Sahlins. Bernie cofounded The Second City along with Paul Sills and Howard Alk and was producer for its first twenty-six years. Beyond Second City, Bernie has produced both television and film and in recent years has done amazing work with new versions of the Mystery Cycles and reinterpreted works of classic theater for the prestigious Chicago Hu-

manities Festival. What follows is an excerpt from Bernie's book Days and Nights at The Second City, *which is not only a fun and interesting memoir of his time at the theater but is a must-read for anyone interested in directing or performing improvisation-based sketch comedy.*

Revue is a stage presentation that uses short scenes of varying lengths. Add music and songs and think of it as generally comical and topical by nature. One can approach this work in many ways, but I do so through the scene as the basic building block. For me the shortest blackout and the funniest song have scenic elements. I define a scene as a short dramatic unit with a beginning, a middle, and an end. As it's used in revue, it is also relevant to the community.

For our work and for that of most of our historical predecessors in revue theater, writers are not usually employed. Most of the material is devised by the cast. Hold on to that idea because it is the focus of much that we will be talking about. But first it would help us to know where we came from, to locate ourselves on a broad, unbroken continuum of theater that stretches back more than twenty-five centuries.

The short comic scene is the oldest form of Western drama. All of us who work in variety, in sitcom, as stand-up comedians, in circuses—all of us who present and devise the comic are the heirs of a great tradition. We have a responsibility to history when we do this work. This is not a form of ancestor worship, just an attempt to keep you from making mistakes that go back twenty-five hundred years.

A dual aspect of human life existed from earliest times. Coupled with the serious cults that worshiped a god, there were the comic cults that laughed at a god. Coupled with serious myths were comic ones. Coupled with heroes were the parodies of heroes. All the serious forms and concepts of human existence were transformed to a comic level.

In the same light we can identify two distinct forms of theater. On the one hand we have that great, serious, classical enterprise, the theater of lofty and noble ideas, of tragic heroes, and of important literary, often poetic, merit. It flourishes when some of the greatest creative and literary minds of an age are drawn to the drama as their means of expression.

But another form of theater flourishes at the same time. It centers on the short comic scene and may be called the popular theater. It is the theater of everyday life, of laughter, of strolling players, clowns, stand-up comedians, vaudeville. It is above all a theater without heroes—strong in satire, parody, and irony. While the classical theater is a recurring but very rare and very short-lived phenomenon, the popular theater has existed in an unbroken line for twenty-six hundred years.

We trace the beginnings of popular theater—in fact of all Western theater—to the sixth century B.C. in Greece. There each year, after the hard work of the harvest, the villagers "unwound" in celebrations that centered on Dionysus, the god of wine. These festivities were raucous, disorderly, irreverent, profane, rude, impudent, and insolent—lots of fun.

Aristotle regarded dramatic comedy as originating in these celebrations, with a differentiation between the leader and the chorus in phallic songs. These songs were featured in the drunken processions that formed part of Dionysian festivals.

From these beginnings a ritual, serious drama branched off. As part of huge religious celebrations, Greek literary figures began to transform the religious and historic myths of their society into what we now know as classical Greek drama. The great theater of Aeschylus, Sophocles, Euripides, and Aristophanes was born. Still, all of their plays, their entire output, were written in a period of fifty-eight years. Think of it! What is more, this great Greek canon, created in just six decades in the fifth century B.C., continued to play for about a hundred years, then disappeared from the stage for almost fifteen centuries. Imagine if there were no written theater from the fifth century until now and you can begin to appreciate the time spans involved.

The older form of performance, the rough comedy, existed alongside the classical. Rather than seriously dealing with the myths of the community, it burlesqued gods and heroes. While one branch of the Dionysian revels grew into the ritualistic drama, another evolved as a sort of street performance involving jugglers, actors, musicians, and acrobats in cheerfully obscene sketches that lampooned not only the gods but politicians, philosophers, generals, and other public figures. These performers formed traveling troupes and they traveled light. They were vulgar, underpaid, and irreverent. And they proved to be the most imperishable form of theater. While the classical theater died and was reborn several times, the popular theater existed without interruption to the present day.

The rough improvisations of the Greek traveling players were transformed into literature with the plays of Aristophanes and Menander. These begot the Roman Plautus, who himself, after centuries of strolling players and troubadours, was reborn in the Italian Renaissance. Then, from Italy in the sixteenth century comedy troupes traveled to Paris and London and became the rage. Molière and Beaumarchais, Shakespeare and Ben Jonson learned from them. Royalty took them up. High and low alike adored them.

But by the end of the seventeenth century these comedians had lost both royal patronage and intellectual approval. They and the comic types they had created survived only in fairs as street players and in a late-eighteenth-century development: the circus. A little over a hundred years ago they returned to the theater in France in a style called vaudeville. And with the advent of the movies and television, with Chaplin, Laurel and Hardy, the Marx Brothers, Jackie Gleason, Robin Williams, John Belushi, and Bill Murray, the theater without heroes flourishes once more. Once more the comedian is king.

We are heirs to a great tradition. And most of us honor that tradition, remaining vulgar, underpaid, and irreverent. I enjoin you to hold on to two of those three qualities.

—Bernard Sahlins

The first version I saw of "An Improvisational Almanac" was two stapled mimeographed pages of inspirational quotes about improvisation belonging to a classmate of mine. She said she had gotten it from another student named Jonathan Pitts, who had edited his improvisational class notes and "published" them. I borrowed her copy and found it fascinating, with lots of insights I agreed with and some I didn't. When we were talking about what a Second City book about improvisation should be, I immediately flashed on Jonathan's almanac both as inspiration for the format and as content. Jonathan Pitts is now the producer of the highly successful Chicago Improv Festival and he teaches at The Second City Training Center. The current version of the almanac is much longer than two pages typed and you'll see portions of it throughout the rest of the book.

AN IMPROVISATIONAL ALMANAC: PART ONE

This is not a list of rules. This is a helpful guideline that has been compiled and reworked to give you, the aspiring artist, assistance in becoming the best you can be. Your instincts and talent should be your first guideline. These suggestions should help you understand how some of the more successful improvisers made the discoveries that led to their success. Some of these guidelines may appear to contradict themselves but then so do many things in life.

To improvise is to expand and heighten the discoveries in the moment.

⇝ ⇝ ⇝

Avoid preconceived ideas. Start each improv like a blank canvas waiting to be covered with details.

⇝ ⇝ ⇝

Always agree; never deny verbal or physical realities.

⇝ ⇝ ⇝

Follow the leader; lead so that others may follow.

⇝ ⇝ ⇝

Silence creates tension. Don't be afraid of this white space; let it happen by using the moment to build to the next moment—the logical or, if you wait another moment, a possible illogical one.

⇝ ⇝ ⇝

Move action forward by adding to the last moment, not sideways by trying to wedge your idea into the fray.

⇝ ⇝ ⇝

Always take the active choice.

❧ ❧ ❧

You don't have to try to be funny. Laughter will happen just by your being human; humanity is funny enough.

❧ ❧ ❧

Action begins with the disruption of the normal routine.

❧ ❧ ❧

Be specific.

❧ ❧ ❧

Start in the middle.

❧ ❧ ❧

Play the opposite.

❧ ❧ ❧

Everything is important. Everything matters.

❧ ❧ ❧

Subtlety is not everything. It is everything else.

❧ ❧ ❧

It is your responsibility to justify.

❧ ❧ ❧

"Yes, and" is always better than "No, but" or "No, and" or "Yes, but."

❧ ❧ ❧

Be alert. Listen very hard to everything outside yourself.

❧ ❧ ❧

KISS—keep it seemingly simple.

❧ ❧ ❧

Always play to the top of your intelligence. Know what you really know. Know what you can do. If you truly don't know, play your ignorance. Play and explore what you don't know. Don't let your ignorance, real or imagined, hold you back. Your honesty will help rather than hinder you.

❧ ❧ ❧

Follow your fears; if you are not comfortable with some aspect of your work, try to do it anyway. Your ineptness and courage will be a truer source of entertainment.

❦ ❦ ❦

Don't push a scene. Follow it and add to it.

❦ ❦ ❦

Trust your instincts and intuition. Let your character help guide you through the unknown.

❦ ❦ ❦

Try not to invent. Try to discover.

❦ ❦ ❦

When in doubt and as a last resort try seduction. Try to be aware of seemingly insignificant detail. Your audience sees everything.

❦ ❦ ❦

Try to become a better audience yourself so that you may begin to understand what makes us appreciate a better performance.

❦ ❦ ❦

Less is more.

CHAPTER TWO: PLAYING THE SCENE

Martin

I first met Martin when he was about four and his aunt Jo Forsberg brought him to Playwrights Theatre Club to see a children's theater production of *Little Red Riding Hood* she'd directed. I played the wolf, and the kids were scared of me. After the show the cast would come out into the audience to meet them. I always took off the wolf head and paws before coming out, but Martin was the only audience member who wasn't afraid to come up to me and shake my hand. He said, and since this was nearly fifty years ago, I'm not quoting exactly here, "I kept on saying it's not really a wolf, it's a friend of Aunt Josephine's. So you didn't scare me too much." And then, with great seriousness, he asked, "Do you like scaring people?" I said, "No, not particularly, but that's my job in the play." And Martin said, and these *were* his exact words, "Play is good." At four, he was already Martin. He was never really young, and he would never have been really old.

A few years later Martin took improv classes at Second City with Viola Spolin, with Jo, and with me. As everyone knows, he wasn't funny, but he was totally present to the others onstage with him. At fourteen, he was definitely already Martin.

I was living in New York in the early seventies. One day I was on my way home from a visit to Chicago and found myself on the same plane with Martin, who was just moving there and was in a state bordering on terror. I was about to start a job at the American Academy of Dramatic Arts, the first improv teacher they'd ever hired. It's a two-year program, and I was to teach the second-year students. I'd wanted the first-year students to have some classes too, and because of my talk with Marty on the plane, I got him the job. I knew nothing about his abilities as a teacher, and I'm not sure he did either, but you could just tell it would work, and of course, it did.

I've always been in awe of Martin's ability to care about so many people so completely. As a teacher, he was even beyond caring; he was almost totally selfless. I don't know a student of his from the American Academy, from Players Workshop, from Second City, or from Columbia who didn't feel nurtured by him and who didn't grow as an artist and as a person because of him. That's why turning the Training Center here over to him was an automatic decision. That's why having him as the head of the improv program at Columbia was an automatic decision. His job at Columbia also included holding faculty workshops to teach them how to teach the games by having them play them. They too felt nurtured and helped to grow by Marty. So did I, especially during the many years we taught an acting class together at Columbia and shared and adopted many of each other's teaching methods. That's also when I found out that he was fun to argue with. And isn't it amazing how he never seemed to need a haircut?

—*Sheldon Patinkin*

One of the goals in creating this book was to honor the teachers of the art of improvisation, and who better to honor them than the students who continue to use those lessons in their professional work. Brian Stack studied with Martin de Maat at The Second City Training Center in the mideighties. He later wrote and performed in two revues at The Second City ETC in Chicago before moving to New York to write for Conan O'Brien. I had the privilege to work with Brian when I directed his touring company—an ensemble that also included Brian's wife, Miriam Tolan. As a group they were extremely tall (Brian, Adam McKay, and Neil Flynn are all six feet five inches tall) and immensely talented. It was one of those rare magical companies that occasionally come together while touring for Second City—they didn't really need a director at all. They had their own style, they wrote their own material, and their shows were as good as or better than anything on the Mainstage at the

same time. And they couldn't have been more fun to work with. Brian, in par-
ticular, is one of the quintessential nice guys of Second City. Onstage, Brian is
incredibly quick-witted but also firmly committed to his partner and the
scene in progress, the sort of improviser that Marty loved best.

I was lucky enough to have Martin de Maat as a teacher and director when
I was a student at The Second City Training Center years ago. While I can't
say I knew him as well as I would've liked to, he did make a big impression
on me and I'm very grateful that I got to see him occasionally in the last
few years before he passed away.

I will always remember Martin as a great teacher but his pure love of
the teaching process sticks with me the most. He clearly saw all students as
individuals and he wanted to draw out the best from every one of them, often surprising the students and himself in doing so. He gave his students
the crucial "freedom to fail" that always makes for the best work. As any
improviser knows, if you can take chances without the fear of being
judged, you're more likely to improve and expand as a performer. Martin
understood that as well as any teacher I've known. The brilliant teacher
and director Mick Napier calls Martin the "poster boy for process" and I
agree completely.

Even Martin's attempts to discipline his class had a unique touch to
them. I remember that when we were putting together our Level 5 show,
Martin would fine us each a dollar if we were late for class. He made it
clear, however, that, when the level finished up, we would use all the money
he'd collected to go out for beers. He managed to encourage us to be responsible while still retaining a spirit of camaraderie and fun. That's a
tough thing to do but it seemed very easy for Martin.

I'll never forget the night that our Level 5 show finished up. Martin's
eyes were very watery and he said to me, "There's never enough time." He
always wanted to give his students one more lesson, one more boost in
confidence, one more revelation of what they could do. He may not have
had the time to do everything he wanted to do as a teacher or director but
those of us who were lucky enough to know and study with him will always be grateful.

In terms of advice/memorable exercises from Martin, a couple come to
mind:

Martin once had us get up and deliberately do the worst improv we could possibly do. I remember one guy in my class starting a scene by saying to his partner, "This is a planet where only I can talk!" and the other person replying, "That's not true, asshole, now stand on your head and speak Latin!" I think that exercise really stuck with me partly because it reinforced the right moves while "requiring" the worst ones. I think the fact that we all had so much fun helped cement the lessons in my memory too.

Another exercise that I remember very well involved each student being assigned an animal to embody. At first, we simply behaved like the animals but then Martin asked us to retain certain traits of our animals as we transitioned into human characters for scenes. It was hilarious and enlightening to see how a "pigeon-like" checkout lady might respond to a "gorilla-like" customer or to see how a "snake-like" husband lies to his "mongoose-like" wife. That exercise taught me that while we often see animals as "beneath us," we're really not too far off. I also learned how important a character's physicality can be in conveying his or her personality to an audience. I know I'll never be very physical as a performer (I think I bend my knees every fifth performance or so) but I know how important and powerful physicality can be to an actor or improviser. Martin's animal exercise was my first real taste of that.

—*Brian Stack*

Perfect Partner

Martin was artistic director of The Second City Training Center in Chicago from 1985 until he died of complications from AIDS in January 2001. Martin was my teacher, my colleague, and my very dear friend. I think what I'll remember the most about Marty was that when he was with a student he was wholly present to that particular human being, giving 150 percent of what he had to offer. At The Second City Training Center when the results of the Level 2 auditions were posted Martin would sit in the little dark staircase between the Mainstage and the ETC theaters and talk to all the students who had not passed the audition. He'd spend enormous amounts of time with each one, talking them through their disappointment. By the time he was done not only would the students feel better about the audition, but Martin would have convinced them that not passing into Level 2 that term was the best thing that could have ever happened to them.

What follows is an excerpt from a transcript of a class taught by Martin in 1986. The class is being side-coached through a space walk exercise, walking around the room with awareness of the space that surrounds them.

As you are walking, make eye contact with people. You don't know their names and you really don't know who they are, but just make eye contact with them. And now, hold the eye contact to the point where it becomes uncomfortable for you, and then look away. [Looking away] is absolutely okay, we all have our threshold. That threshold will always exist in a nonfamiliar place. Just notice where the threshold is, where the intimacy barrier is. You can make eye contact, hold it for three seconds, that's normal, and then you move away. Just notice the moment where the "fear" comes up and you have the freedom to go; you don't have to hold eye contact beyond the point where it is uncomfortable for you.

Now, when you make eye contact with someone, notice the intimacy threshold, and hold the eye contact a few seconds longer than is comfortable for you. Do it for just a couple of extra seconds and then go on to someone else. Start discovering that the space beyond our intimacy threshold or beyond the point where we start feeling intruded upon is also safe. The arenas beyond our fears are safe once they become familiar.

Just be honest with yourself. You can't fail here. There is no way to fail. If you can only hold eye contact for half a second, then try to hold it for a whole second and go. You're fine.

Now, get yourself to face a partner. Make eye contact with that person and notice when the intimacy threshold hits and it becomes uncomfortable for you. Then what I want you to do is to singularly focus on having your partner have success at holding the eye contact. Not you, your partner. Exist for your partner to have success. You exist for me so that I have success and I exist for you so that you have success. Is it becoming easier? (General yeses.)

That's the bottom line of this work. The bottom line is that if you want to have success, then what you do is you get out of your own bullshit and you exist for someone outside of yourself. We all have a certain amount of

Relationship Exercises

SIMULTANEOUS SCENES EXPLORING RELATIONSHIP: *Number of Players.* This classroom or rehearsal exercise is designed to be done in pairs simultaneously.

To Play. Each pair chooses a simple activity that can be carried on throughout the entire exercise—say, washing dishes. They play a one-minute scene in which the characters do not know each other. Then continue with the same activity and performers but play characters with a long history.

Next, each plays a simple one-minute transaction scene; one player is the buyer and the other a seller or vendor. Do the same scene again, but this time add that the characters are the bitterest mortal enemies.

Finally, pick a location and play two strangers. For the first minute, both characters are completely indifferent to each other. Continue the scene for another minute but now have the characters be intensely affected by each other—they may not know why but they should feel a strong pull toward or a strong aversion to their partner.

Notice how each change affected the scene. What was more fun to play? Which scene do you think would be more fun for an audience to watch? While one common improv "rule" is that characters should know each other, my students have often found that the most interesting scene both to play and watch was the second half of the "stranger" scene. At this point, I often go back and have my

garbage that we live our lives in, a certain number of beliefs about ourselves: "I'm too old." "My hair's too curly." "I'm too thin." So if we get out beyond ourselves and we exist for someone outside of ourselves, what we have is success. Because you are at your best when you are functioning for someone other than yourself.

Focus on your partner. I swear to you that's how you do this.

—*Martin de Maat*

Relationship

From the early Second City scenes such as "First Affair," in which Severn Darden's professorial father confronts Barbara Harris's intellectually precocious teen about her first sexual experience, to more recent scenes such as Wicked, in which Tina Fey and Rachel Dratch played mother and daughter discussing a much more up-to-date version of the same subject in a Boston mall, the relationship has driven some of the best scenes on our stages. Shari Hollett is an instructor and director at our theater in Toronto. In addition to her work with Second City, she is active in the Toronto theater community. In fact, I first met her when she and her husband, Chris Earle, brought to Chicago Big Head Goes to Bed, *their play about how life with a toddler affects the relationship between a husband and wife.*

Do you remember how, as a child, if you thought too hard about breathing you felt unable to do it? The same applies to improv. You cannot constantly think about what you are doing while doing it. To have the true mind/body connection that is needed for good improv, you must be in the moment. Equally important is your connection to the person or people in the scene with you. This is called relationship. Without it there is no scene.

Relationships in improv, like relationships in real life, comprise all the connections (emotional, physical, familial, and hierarchical) that can exist between characters. As in life, relationships are a source of both great pain and great comedy—sometimes both at the same time. Human beings are defined by their desperate need to connect with one another, and at the same time they find it incredibly difficult to do so. The gap between our desire for connection and our inability to communicate with each other makes for great comic relationships.

Character and Relationship—Two Sides of the Same Coin

Character and relationship can be a chicken-and-egg scenario. Which comes first? Characters don't exist in a vacuum; they are defined by their relationships. And vice versa. In preparing for a scene you might start with relationship, and then move on to the specifics of character:

> HE: For this scene, let's be brother and sister.
> SHE: I'll be the glamorous big sister trying to get ready for a big date.
> HE: And I'll be your little brother pestering you with questions about sex.

Or you might start with characters and then find a relationship for them:

> SHE: I want to play a flamboyant flamenco dancer.
> HE: I want to play an eccentric war veteran.
> SHE: Let's make them teacher and student. I'll be teaching you how to dance the flamenco.

Whichever you begin with, and whether you pre-plan or make your choices on the fly, the relationship is the foundation for everything that happens between the characters onstage. How clearly you define and explore that relationship determines the success of the scene.

As in all good improv, the best way to establish relationship is by showing, not telling. Body language, physical proximity, activity, and tone of voice can tell us as much about a relationship as what the characters say to each other. It's amazing how much you can show without any dialogue at all. Take the example of a simple two-person scene: a man and a woman are sitting on a park bench, holding hands, smiling giddily, staring at each other with a sense of wonder. We can assume they are young lovers. Perhaps they slowly unwrap and eat sandwiches. Are they coworkers on a lunch break? They amorously feed each other bits of food, and then quickly look around to see if they are being observed. Are they having an affair? The scene has only just begun, not a word has been spoken, but we've already learned a lot. As the scene progresses, it's what they say, how they say it, what they do, and how they do it that tells us what kind of a young couple they are.

students perform scenes in which the characters both know each other and are strongly affected by each other. In most cases, these are the strongest of all of the scenes because the relationship is the most interesting and vivid.

REITERATION: *To Play.* Set up a simple Who, What, Where. Before each player can speak she must repeat the last sentence or so of the previous player. Slight paraphrasing is fine, especially to retain the sense of the scene; for example:

> A: . . . I never want to see you again.
> B: You never want to see me again. That's a terrible thing to say.
> A: That is a terrible thing to say, but I mean it nonetheless.
> B: You mean it nonetheless.
> A: I mean it nonetheless.

It is perfectly fine to simply repeat your partner's line; there is no mandate that you must add to it. You must, however, repeat the very last thing your partner said, not the second-to-last thing, as is sometimes a temptation.

While this exercise is also useful for working on "Yes, and . . . ," it is especially useful for relationship work. The repetition forces players to respond to everything said. It is very difficult to have those responses and not have the characters be strongly affected by each other, thus building relationship.

CONTACT OR TOUCH TO SPEAK: *To Play.* Set up a simple Who, What, Where. Before a player may speak he must initiate physical contact with his partner. Each new interaction must begin with a new point of contact—no fair just holding hands for the entire scene. You also must maintain contact for the duration of the time you are speaking—if you or your partner pulls away, then you must fall silent. Work to justify the contact within the context of the scene; find your reason for initiating each new contact.

Most improvisers quickly discover that the only way to make contact scenes make sense is to play characters whose relationship or situation is extremely intimate or intense.

EYE CONTACT TO SPEAK: *To Play.* Set up your scene as you do in Contact or Touch to Speak. In this variation, instead of physically touching you must have direct eye contact with your partner in order to speak. Be sure to hold eye contact for the duration of speech, but don't just spend the entire scene glued to each other's eyes. Try to maintain an environment filled with objects and activity.

As in Contact, relationship must come to the fore because we need our scene partner in order to proceed; it is impossible to "make" the scene happen without his or her active participation. Eye contact has an additional benefit of keeping the scene in the present; when we are making up a story or remembering something from the past, we tend to look up and to the right.

Environment is also a crucial part of this physical exploration of relationship, since we associate certain relationships with certain environments. We see two people typing side by side; we assume they are coworkers in an office. They are working very intently, and are repeatedly checking on each other's progress. We realize they are rivals, trying to outdo each other as the fastest typist. Already we have the beginnings of an interesting relationship.

If a scene begins with a man and a woman reading in bed, we see a couple, but what else can the actors show us? Without even speaking they can clearly paint a picture of an unhappy relationship. They might struggle for control of the duvet or fight for space on the bed. This can be shown before they even speak; imagine the possibilities when they actually begin to communicate verbally in support of that vivid physical relationship. The more specific the physical choices are, the more defined the relationship will be.

Do I Know You?

When deciding on relationship the improviser has a simple but crucial choice to make: do the characters know each other or are they strangers? Both options have their advantages. Characters with a shared history—either as friends, family, coworkers, or lovers—can draw upon that history in the scene. You can use this history as either an engine of conflict—"The last time you took me out to dinner, Nixon was still president"—or as a way to bring characters closer together—"You're even more beautiful now than the day we met in that plastic surgeon's office."

Giving your characters a history is also a way to instantly raise the stakes in your scene. The longer you've known someone, the more likely it is that you've invested emotionally in that relationship—for better or worse. The people you're close to are the ones most likely to drive you crazy, and they're also the ones who can hurt you the most. Either way the stakes are sky high. And the more the characters have to lose, the more the audience has to gain.

Let's look at another example. Perhaps you've agreed to try a father-and-daughter scene at a beach, but that's all you've set up. How the scene will unfold and what this father and daughter's relationship is like is up to both of you. If you are listening (probably the number one rule of improv), your partner will give you lots of hints as to what kind of father or daughter you are. How you build on these is your shared responsibility.

If the actress playing the daughter enters and says, "Now before you say anything, I thought this thong bikini was a one-piece when I bought it," we can make certain assumptions about their relationship—the father in the past has been stern and conservative; the daughter spins the truth to suit herself. The actor playing the father has many options here: he can be aghast as she expects, or he can try to be "like the kids" and reveal that he is also sporting a thong, or he can burst into tears and scream, "My little girl is becoming a woman." The only thing he can't do is ignore her endowment of him. She has given their relationship the gift of past history. If he ignores the offer, he is denying the relationship and the scene will likely get stuck as they struggle for control. Every choice you make should have an impact on the other person and help us continue to define relationship.

Playing strangers can also make for great scenes. Since there's no shared history, the characters and the audience all begin with the same amount of information: none. The fun here is watching a new relationship take shape in front of us. As in real life, the relationship between strangers is very fluid: the characters have no history to draw on, no entrenched roles to play out. Instead they are constantly asking themselves, Who is this other person? Are they friend or foe? What do they think of me? Am I making a good impression? How can I get what I want from them? Watching two strangers discover just how much or how little they have in common and seeing them struggle to get what they want from each other can be endlessly entertaining.

Relationships from Real Life

In order to be specific and detailed (as all good actors and especially improvisers must be), you have to become an expert in human nature. You get to do for research what most people do for fun: "people-watch." You must be a sort of amateur anthropologist—observing and noting the mysteries and idiosyncrasies of Homo sapiens, so that you can create characters and relationships drawn from real life as opposed to pale imitations of characters from movies or TV. Base your characters and relationships in truth—the audience will reward you for it.

This research allows you to bring real life to the stage through your un-

TWO-CHARACTER HOT SEAT INTERVIEW:
To Play. In this classroom or rehearsal variation on character interviews, two players are seated onstage together. They are interviewed in character about their relationship—how they met, how they spend their time together, and so on. Interviewers should begin by alternating questions to give each player a chance to build the history of the relationship and then gradually relax and let the two players take control of the interaction, telling their mutual story.

This exercise is a great way to move out of cliché and discover rich textured relationships with interesting histories. One variation that reinforces this is to begin with a traditional "boring" relationship such as doctor/patient or husband/wife. You can also do this exercise with three or even more players.

derstanding of people. By interacting with other actors who are working from their own level of reference, together you can create funny and complex relationships.

Objectives and Emotion

If your goal is to create real characters in real situations you must acknowledge their objectives. In all scenes characters are driven by their wants and their needs. These may be quite simple but they become extremely important when playing out the scene. Characters all need something from each other.

The daughter at the beach needs to be understood. She attempts this through wanting approval from her father. The father needs to be needed and wants his daughter to show him he is by listening to him.

The wife in the bedroom needs to feel appreciated and wants attention from her husband. The husband needs to be respected for who he is and not for who his wife wants him to be; he wants to be allowed to read his paper without feeling guilty.

The coworker in the office needs to feel important and wants his colleague to feel jealous of his accomplishments.

In analyzing wants and needs it is important to pick active objectives; you may need love but what you want from the other person in the scene is more specific. You may want forgiveness from them or a promotion, a hug, understanding, or compassion. They in turn want something from you. Of course as people we often have trouble asking for what we really want so we use a series of what we call tactics to meet our individual objectives: "I will try being nice to you in hopes that you will also be nice to me." But define *nice;* perhaps your version of nice is completely irritating to me. Again an understanding of human behavior (including your own) will greatly assist you.

Making emotional offers is a key to defining relationship. When you see characters have emotional impact on each other you assume certain things about their relationship. For example, an actor enters the stage and begins the activity of preparing a meal; a second actor enters and the first actor drops what she is doing and runs to him, embraces him, on the verge of tears, and says, "I thought you'd never come back." Again the possibilities are endless: a son returning from war, a husband returning from a business trip, a newlywed returning from the bathroom. The one thing we know is that their relationship is of an intimate nature. The specifics are up to the actors.

When you enter the world of relationship you enter the world of possibility. By using your cultural and social awareness, and by tapping into physicality, emotional context, past history, and objectives, you and your fellow actors will bring your scenic relationships to vivid life.

—*Shari Hollett*

Transformation of Relationships

Avery Schreiber was in one of the earliest Second City casts. His partnership with Jack Burns took him to California, first working with the Committee in San Francisco and later to television and film work in Los Angeles. To a certain generation of TV watcher, he is best known for a series of Dorito's commercials. To performers in Los Angeles, he was known as a premier teacher of improvisation. I had the great good fortune to attend a master class with Avery a few years ago; he had a true gift for understanding and communicating the complex mysteries that lie in the most simple of the beginning exercises. In particular, Avery was a master of transformation in improvisation. Avery died while this book was being written but his wife (and former Second City waitress), Shelley, graciously has allowed us to reprint some portions of the syllabi for his classes in Los Angeles.

Viola Spolin's game Transformation of Relationships is a game that I feel is the peak ultimate of the Spolin games. I may feel this way because Dick Schaal and I were the first ones she had try it. We had been doing Transformation of Objects and had a lot of fun with Transformation of the Where when she wondered aloud if Transformation of the Who was a possible game. She could see it in her magically creative imagination and explained it to us quickly. Dick and I understood her theory and jumped at the chance to show her.

For almost four years Dick and I played it every night before Second City audiences. We had one unbroken rule in all that time: no cop-outs! If a particularly hysterical scene happened to evolve from the shifting interplay, we could work on it in regular workshops, not repeat it if something similar suddenly reappeared.

One wondrous side issue that we both acknowledged was the obvious extrasensory aspect of the experience. We both shared prolonged moments of what seemed to us to be telepathic levels of communication. So attuned were we to the other's sensibility that when I turned around as a chair-toting whip-snapping lion tamer, he would come out of his spin as a roaring lion! Both would note our amazement at the many times we had this experience.

TRANSFORMATION OF RELATIONSHIPS: *To Play.* The suggestion taker explains the nature of the game.

> SUGGESTION TAKER: Now we would like to do a game for you that we call Transformations. In it, the players start with two characters and then through a series of transformations they end up as two totally different ones. In order to do it we would like you to suggest two characters to begin with.
>
> AUDIENCE MEMBER: A monk and a nun!
>
> SUGGESTION TAKER: Very good, they will start with a monk and a nun. Then they will go through a series of transformations (other characters), and then, so we know when the game is over, we need a suggestion from you as to the final characters you would like to see.
>
> AUDIENCE MEMBER: Frankenstein!
>
> SUGGESTION TAKER: Excellent! They will start with a monk and a nun and end up with Frankenstein!

The players start moving around the stage, mirroring or not, watching each other until the monk or nun emerges from the movement. They play a short scene between these two and then watch for points of divergence that allow new transformations to occur. When the Frankenstein opportunity occurs they launch into it and the lights come down.

(Note: the average length became six minutes and the number of transformations varied according to whether there was a full moon or not.)

—*Avery Schreiber*

Perfect Partner, Part Two

It is your goal to be a perfect partner; are you:

Participating with an open mind?

A nonworrier?

Giving?

Totally accepting of all that your partners do?

Willing to play?

Honest?

Using your intelligence?

Respectful?

Committed?

Supportive?

Creative, trusting, and acting on your instincts and associations?

Courageous?

Comfortable with yourself?

Intuitive with skills?

Exploring and heightening?

Trusting and trustworthy?

Vulnerable?

Energetic?

Versatile?

Unpredictable (creative and courageous in your choices)?

Confident?

Receptive?

Compassionate?

Focused?

Without judgment about yourself or your partner's talent and abilities?

Actively assimilating the above into your way of being?

—Martin de Maat

Status

If I were creating a new lexicon of improv rules I would create three dos to go along with the three don'ts of Story, Questions, and Denial: Give and

Take Focus, Explore and Heighten, and Play Status. The founder of Theatresports, Keith Johnstone, defined the use of status as an improvisational technique. Keith was brought in to teach some workshops at The Second City Chicago in the mideighties and trained some of our Canadian faculty with his group Loose Moose in Ontario, but it would be stretching it to say that we have any claim on him or his work. What follows isn't strictly Johnstone; it is my own interpretation of his ideas as it has evolved through my work with improvisers in The Second City Training Center. If you are interested in exploring more deeply I highly recommend Johnstone's books *Impro* and *Impro for Storytellers.*

In a nutshell, status is a set of physical and verbal behaviors we use to determine where someone is in the social pecking order of the moment. All social animals have some set of these behaviors. Try the eye contact game with your pet—stare into his eyes until one of you looks away. Your dog should look away first, acknowledging your dominance in the household. If he doesn't, you have some major dog problems on your hands.

When I teach status in my classes at Second City I caution students to be aware of several issues. First, we shouldn't confuse status with social class—status is behavioral and can be altered moment to moment. Thus a beggar can grovel for spare change (low status) one moment, and the next will verbally abuse the man who passed him by without giving a handout (high status). Secondly, certain status behaviors are not intrinsically good or bad—it all depends on the context. Depending on the situation, high-status behaviors can be perceived as aggressive or even rude, or they can be seen as paternal or confident. Low status may appear polite or warm in one case and weak, servile, or awkward in another. Finally, status rarely exists in a vacuum; we are continually playing status games with each other—dropping status to raise someone else, or lowering another's status to raise ourselves up.

For improvisers, status provides any number of valuable tools. The Status game is an easy and specific one that can be played in any scene. It adds verisimilitude to our work; even if our audiences have never heard of the term *status,* they recognize the human behavior it creates onstage. Status takes us out of our heads and into our bodies. It gives the improviser a concrete physical way to respond to action in an improvisational scene, to show instead of tell. For example, in an office scene a secretary speaks up for herself in the face of an abusive boss. Her status rises and she shows it by squaring her shoulders and raising her chin. The boss shakes his head in confusion, stutters. We can actually see his status fall.

Using status helps avoid the pitfall of argument in a scene. Conflict in a scene can turn to argument when both players are trying too hard to "win" the scene for their character. Scenes get stuck in argument; there is no forward motion. It's like a staged combat in which each participant just stands throwing punches at the other. If we use status to "take the punch," the scene takes on movement—there are now winners and losers.

Status is the source of a great deal of comedy. Once you become aware of status, you can see it in every comedic tradition. Pretty much universally, humans find it funny when someone drops status. Hence the classic pie in the face or slipping on a banana peel. Stage and film comedies are full of comic characters whose status behavior doesn't match their occupation or social class—the low-status king, a high-status butler. In an improvised scene we can mine this rich source; getting laughs through our interactions with our partners can be much easier than coming up with witty references.

Use the list of status behaviors in the appendix and the following exercises to explore using status in your improvisation.

EYE CONTACT: *To Play.* This is the classroom exercise I use when I introduce status to my classes. I begin by having the entire class walk around the room for a minute or so, making eye contact with their classmates as they pass them. I ask them to silently check in with themselves as they make eye contact. How do they feel? How do they feel about the person they are making eye contact with? Then I instruct one-half of the group to hold eye contact as they walk around the room, to really hold eye contact for as long as they can, and then to look away and not to look back. The other half of the class is told to make eye contact, look down at their own shoes, and then to look back. After about a minute or so I have them switch roles, so that those who were holding eye contact now break it and those who were breaking eye contact hold it. Throughout this process students are encouraged to continue checking in. How do they feel now? How have their feelings changed? Then, I take about thirty seconds of walking with eye contact back to normal, which is usually accompanied by audible sighs of relief from the class. This exercise allows students to immediately experience what status is and how it affects them physically and emotionally.

SILENT MOVIE STATUS: *To Play.* These are two-person, one-minute scenes that start with the suggestion of a simple Where. Players interact using the given status parameters but may not speak—characters should not be struck dumb and forced to resort to mime, but just function in silence. Characters should know each other. The goal here is awareness of status as a physical behavior.

> 1. Both start at a similar status and try to get their status higher than that of their partner. (Note: in this particular setup, players must stay in connection with each other. It is possible to "win" by ignoring your partner throughout the entire scene, but it doesn't teach us much in the exercise.)
>
> 2. Both start at a similar status and try to get their status lower than that of their partner.
>
> 3. One starts high and one starts low; they play with this status differential until the instructor says, "Switch," at which point they must abruptly trade status.
>
> 4. One starts high and one starts low. They must work together, gradually switching status so that their status is reversed by the end of the scene.

STATUS SCENES WITH SPEECH: *To Play.* Use the preceding status exercises but add speech. Players should not take status through denial—"I'm your superior officer." "No, you're not."—or through surprise information— "What you don't know is, I just bought this company and now I'm your boss."

REVERSE STATUS CHARACTER SCENES: *To Play.* Start with a classic high-status/low-status relationship such as principal/student or doctor/patient. When you begin the scene, reverse the traditional status—for example, a low-status principal with a high-status student.

Living Large in the Moment

In 1974, Michael Gellman was the youngest person ever to work on Second City's Chicago Mainstage. During his time as a performer he developed a somewhat legendary impression of Richard Nixon, a man many years his senior. Michael has always had the persona of the worldly wise cynic—the one who has been around and seen it all and lived to tell the tale. Michael taught me to drink single-malt scotch, got me a job in The Second City box office, and taught me much of what I know and value about improvisation. Now, as my colleague on the senior faculty of the Chicago Training Center, Michael continues to amaze me with the depth and breadth of his knowledge about the improvisational art form. Michael's understanding of improvisation is truly that of an artist; he moves beyond the simple rules and strategies of beginners and penetrates the mysterious processes that transform serviceable improvisation into something deeper.

I was introduced to improvisation in the late 1960s. Ron Douglas had left The Second City Touring Company and joined the cast of Dudley Riggs's Brave New Workshop in Minneapolis. Ron taught beginning-level weekly workshops using methods he had learned at The Second City in Chicago. The method he used was based on Viola Spolin's book *Improvisation for the Theater*. Viola's book was and is the bible for improvisational training.

One of the ideas stressed in Viola's work is the use of the Where. Improvisers generally perform on a bare stage and must create their environment and the objects in that environment using mime. The student/actor first learns that the empty stage is filled with space/air and that space can be molded and shaped to create anything the improviser can imagine. The student goes from creating objects out of space, to creating imaginary environments out of space, to eventually creating activity in the Where. By creating activity the improvisational actor shows objects (props), defines the environment (setting), and shows his character to the audience.

As an example, the actor might get the suggestion of a soup kitchen. She might start by stirring soup in a large industrial-size soup pot. With a few moves, she can show us many things in the Where. Turning a knob creates a stove under the soup pot. When she adds a spice she gets from a cupboard or takes a towel from a drawer, the soup kitchen begins to appear before our eyes. We also see how she moves through the space quickly or slowly, happy or sad, and a character begins to emerge. With the simplest activities—stirring soup, adding spice, and getting a towel—she creates for the audience a Who (character), Where (soup kitchen), and What (making soup).

One of the key mantras in improvisational theater is "Show—don't tell." We try not to tell a story but rather to dramatize the story. We are taught that the first thing to do when improvising a scene is to start with an activity (stirring soup). But is this the best way to create action? As we began to explore different applications for improvisation, the idea of starting with an activity became a hindrance rather than a help.

Not only did our techniques have to change, so did our terminology. We began to make a very firm distinction between response and reaction. When the actor responds to what just happened onstage, he tends to be making a conscious choice. A response tends to be verbal and emotionally unconnected, to put clever before character. On the other hand, when the actor reacts to what just happened onstage, he tends to be emotionally driven. A reaction is connected emotionally and physically before it is verbalized and puts the truth of the character before the cleverness of the actor. It is my belief that if an audience walks out of the theater talking about the actors—"I liked the tall one," "I liked the short one"—we have failed. But if they walk out talking about the characters—"I like the scene with the two brothers"—we have succeeded.

In the early 1980s, while acting as artistic director for The Second City Toronto, I began to work on what we called "long-form" improvisation: sustaining a character for an extended period of time. Years before, Del Close, our director at The Second City Chicago, challenged me with a simple but provocative "What if?" It should be possible, he said, to improvise a play of literary quality by night, transcribe it, and send it off to Samuel French for publication in the morning.

In Toronto, I had the opportunity to conduct weekly workshops where we explored the possibility of creating improvised one-act plays. We found that we could create long-form pieces of theater with a single suggestion from the audience of a Where. The problem was finding new ways of improvising. The tried-and-true methods of Viola Spolin and Second City worked very well for creating short scenic material used in comedy revue but felt limited for longer, more dramatic material. Early on we realized that in order for the improviser to sustain a character for more than a few minutes, we had to do what an actor in a text play could do: live moment to moment.

The standard way of beginning scenes with an activity seemed to encourage the actor/improviser to make a choice. The audience would suggest "soup kitchen" and the actor would decide to start stirring a pot of soup. The question became, if we start with a conscious choice by the actor, can the character be truly living in the moment? Does making a conscious choice diminish our ability to improvise spontaneously moment to moment? We had to develop new techniques in order to create long-form improvisation. The idea of trading activity for discovery in the Where helped us understand how to improvise more effectively in the moment.

We started to understand that improvisation could be thought of as a process of working backward, not forward. It is not about thinking what comes next, the next line or funny bit. If the improviser is paying attention to what was just said or the last moment and reacts to it, she is living in the present.

Viola defines spontaneity as "a moment of explosion; a free moment of self-expression." When we talk about moment-to-moment improvisation or "living in the moment" we are referring to what we think of as good improvisation. In fact, we think of living in the moment as a key to good improvisation.

A moment can be many things in a variety of situations, but for teaching and directing actors I have found it useful to define a moment as the space between discovery and reaction. The amount of time it takes between the moment of discovery and the moment of reaction can be less than a second, or if you're courageous enough, several minutes. A good improviser is said to be always in the moment. When an actor is living in the moment, his work is at its best.

Let's break that idea down. The first part is the discovery. The character can walk into the Where and decide on an activity or make a discovery. Let's go back to the soup kitchen. The activity was to stir soup but there are dozens of possible discoveries. If the actor is to avoid a conscious decision she must make a discovery. I encourage students to embrace the first thing they see. The discovery can be anything in the Where: an object, something on the walls, something outside the window, music playing, a smell, anything at all. We call the discovery a point of concentration (POC).

The second part of the moment is that time between the discovery and the reaction. This is most often purely physical. For example, we see a couple sitting at a café table. He produces a ring box, opens it, and slides it across the table toward the woman. She drops her head, chin on her chest, then slowly raises her head to look the young man in the eye. We know from observing people that her reaction is probably going to be negative.

The third step is the reaction. It is often verbal and must be a direct link to the emotion resulting from the discovery. Again, the actor should not be making a conscious choice separate from the discovery. The woman in the café raises her eyes and says, "George, you've got to be kidding."

Many of you might consider the woman's head move to be the first part of her reaction. I separate the moment between her discovery (the ring box) and her verbal reaction ("George, you've got to be kidding") in order to allow the students/actors to understand how we humans truly behave and to be able to reproduce that behavior. Too often, improvisers tend to forget the middle beat—the physical. They tend to go up in their heads, trying desperately to find the "right" thing to say. We should allow for a moment of emotion so the reaction itself becomes a discovery, not a choice. If we slow down a film of human interaction, we can usually tell what someone is going to say before they say it. People tend to physicalize their emotion before they verbalize it, and in fact if we break it down, the physical might be one emotion and the verbal another. For example, the woman in the café drops her head then raises her eyes and, trying to sound happy through her clenched teeth, says, "Yes, George, I'd love to marry you, honestly."

The other reason to focus on the moment between discovery and reaction at Second City is because that is where the comedy is found. How and why and for how long that moment is used is the science of comedic timing. We might not be able to teach people how to be funny, but we can teach them comic delivery.

The best part of developing new techniques for long-form improvisation was that they seemed to be very well suited for training actors in text work. One of my goals was to create a bridge between improvisers and actors. The Couch exercise is a good example of where we are headed. It addresses the ideas of reaction versus response, playing moment to moment as well as the similarities in training for both the improvisational and text actor.

THE COUCH: This exercise was developed by accident while teaching a scene study class at Act One Studios in Chicago. Two student actors were having a hard time playing a scene moment to moment. They were rushing to their dialogue without exploring the possibilities of the scene's opening moments.

To Play. The setup is relatively simple but there is a lot to explore when you break it down. The Where is an apartment with a couch center stage, an entrance stage right, and a table stage left. The Who is two actors: character A is on the couch and character B is offstage right ready to enter. The action of the scene is described for the student actors before the scene starts. Character A, who is on the couch, makes a discovery inside the apartment. Character B enters with a bag of groceries stage right and stops. Character A has a line of dialogue in reaction to his discovery, then character B crosses upstage of the couch, puts the groceries on the table stage left, and turns and delivers her line, which is, "I brought the groceries home."

The Couch can be split into two beats of discovery to reaction. The first is the person on the couch (character A). Character A must make a discovery in the environment (the Where) and physically react to that discovery as character B enters. Character A then delivers his verbal reaction (a line of dialogue) as character B stands stage right of the couch.

The second beat is character B's turn. Character B's discovery is whatever character A just said. Her discovery is character A's reaction (line of dialogue). The moment between discovery and reaction for character B is a long one. Character B must cross from stage right to stage left with a bag of groceries, place the groceries on the table, and turn and deliver her reaction line: "I brought the groceries home."

During that entire moment between character B's discovery to character A's reaction line and saying, "I brought the groceries home," character B must be holding the emotion felt when she heard character A's line; not up in her head, thinking about what to say when she puts the groceries down.

THE TOWN GAME (LA RONDE): Michael created the Town Game exercise while working on various forms designed to create improvised one-act plays. As is true with many of the best improvisational games and exercises, something similar with another name, La Ronde, was making the rounds in other improvisational circles at about the same time. La Ronde refers to the way that the scenic structure mimics that of the Arthur Schnitzler play of the same name.

Number of Players. Six (but can accommodate anywhere between four and eight)

Suggestions. Six locations that one would find in a small town—for example, the hardware store or under the bleachers at the high school football stadium

To Play. In the first round of play, one scene takes place in each location. Each player does two scenes—players A and B perform a scene together, followed by a scene between players B and C, and on in the same manner until players F and A do a scene together. Scenes are thirty seconds long and silent—characters are silent because they choose to be and not because they have been struck dumb and must communicate via sign language. Each player maintains the same character throughout the entire exercise using the discoveries they make about themselves and their character's relationship with their first scene partner to inform their work in the next scene.

In the second round, scenes are one minute long. Players may speak but should avoid discussing the events of the previous scenes—it's a small town, so we assume that everyone already knows everyone else's business. In the version Michael first taught me, this round was one word at a time.

In the third round, scenes are two to three minutes long, depending of the needs of the scene. Players should be encouraged to maintain moment-to-moment response and not to put their attention on plot. It's easy to get hooked on the soap opera aspect of the exercise but if the players stay in the moment and make their discoveries, the plot somehow miraculously takes care of itself.

While performing this exercise in a class I had one of those epiphanies we are lucky enough to have on occasion, where suddenly something you have heard a million times becomes real and concrete and you say to yourself, "Of course, that's the way to do it, it's obvious." While obvious, it is simultaneously the most difficult part of improvising for many of us to fully comprehend—that the best way to improvise is to take our focus off our brains and ourselves and let our bodies and their responses take over.

For those of you who might want to use this exercise in your workshop, here are some thoughts:

After two actors do the exercise once, have them switch roles with a new set of discoveries.

Make sure character A's first line is a true reaction to the discovery and not simply a description of the discovery. Do not allow storytelling with a line of accusation toward character B.

At the end of the exercise, allow the other students to decide what they thought the relationship was between character A and character B.

Before character B enters, the actor can make a discovery and have an emotional reaction to "what's beyond" the living-room area. When she carries that emotion into the scene, be sure character B's emotion changes with character A's first line.

After the last line ("I brought the groceries home"), hold the scene to allow character A on the couch to have a second beat of reaction to discovery.

When the scene is done well, the audience will not notice the use of discovery to reaction instead of activity. However, the final product will be better theater because activity is actor driven and reaction is character driven. The idea of changing the opening of a scene to a discovery instead of an activity is only one technique we employed to achieve the improvised one-act play. It is an example of where improvisational performance and training might go in the years ahead. I believe improvisation has the potential to live side by side with what we call "the method" but only if we realize that improvisational theater must put the quality of performance before the cleverness of the actor.

—*Michael J. Gellman*

Play Is Physical

Dexter Bullard has made a career of finding and using moments of physical attention and impulse. His theater company Plasticene specializes in abstract physical performance created through improvisation. Additionally, Dexter's work as a director with The Second City Touring Company and at Chicago's ETC theater brought a new awareness of the power of physical play to the work on our stages.

Can we just "play"?
—*Abby Sher to me during a hellish rehearsal of* Better Late Than Nader

The art of improvisation is an art of highly skilled play. And play is physical. This is what I champion over and over again in my classes at the Training Center. There is a strong inertia in improvisers pulling them to stand stiffly four feet apart and trade dialogue—while ensuring that nothing is going on! The sole unit of improv is action. Although it can be tiny, almost undetectable, the presence of action is what keeps an audience watching and players in play. Action is always physical—bodily, energetic, and shared.

Viola Spolin noticed this same problem in her acting classes in the fifties. There wasn't enough playfulness in her players to create vibrant and believable events onstage. She noticed that when a player was placed in front of an audience, his or her natural sense of play magically disappeared into stiffness and indication. To solve the problem, she looked to children. She noticed that children play easily and constantly. Children's games require and elicit boisterous physical action and great imagination. A realization followed: if games create play, and play creates great acting, then games could create great acting. Starting from a collection of children's games written by Neva Boyd, she helped lead the founders of Second City to the creation of a lively, jazz-tinged, superpresent, hilarious, audience-interactive form of satiric theatrical art. We must remember this and remember to play.

Warming Up

In order to encourage physicality in improv, you must raise your players' physicality through a warm-up. Typical improv warm-ups are designed to create energy. This usually means a minute of shaking and jumping around and yelling that just puts players on edge. A warm-up should raise the pulse, necessitate full breathing, warm the muscles, bring active concentration, and then address players physically to a partner. Give your warm-up at least fifteen minutes and do *not* stop except to explain rules briefly. Practice side-coaching to not stop the action. Remember that action breeds action. This is true in scenes as well as in class or rehearsal. One good action results in another. Momentum is the key. You want them to clarify themselves physically in the moment. Then the rest of the class rolls easier. [Exercises marked with an asterisk can be found in Viola Spolin's *Improvisation for the Theater.*]

1. Start with something that raises the pulse and something that involves everyone by themselves—jumping jacks, fast walking without collisions, backward walking, imaginary obstacle course, freeze tag, explosion tag,* air boxing, air guitar, running in place to images (There's a rabid dog after you! Ice cream ahead!), or ideas from any sport or exercise.

2. Move immediately to a stretching form like Rolling on the Floor, Space Substance,* Windmills, Reaching to All Points in the Room, Flowing to the Floor and Back Up, Twists, Large Object Work,* Lunges, Yoga, martial arts forms, and so on.

3. Move immediately to a game that involves everyone's concentration and physical participation; Zip-Zap-Zop, Pass the Clap, Kitty Wants a Corner, Spud, Don't Touch the Floor, Square Dancing, Jump the Stick, Steal the Bacon, British Bulldog, Breathe Together, Move at the Same Time/Freeze at the Same Time, ball games, relay races, or any focused children's game will do. Objects can help here too—pillows, a beanbag chair, balls, sticks, ropes, Nerf toys, hula hoops, cafeteria trays, whatever . . . they will know what to do and create games you never imagined.

4. Move to the same game or new actions played with partners. Let them explore where the action goes between them. They will be creative and not thinking by now. (Note: I do a lot of work with partners improvising simultaneously all together rather than watching each other. This keeps the action going and keeps people out of chairs for longer. I find people can practice this way without per-

formance pressure on all the time.) Segue to verbal/vocal structures like Free Association, Singing Together, ABC, Story Word by Word, Simultaneous Talking, Contrapuntal Argument,* or Questions. Don't let the action die just because they are now using voice. We talk and do things at the same time constantly in life. Don't let the words kill the physical life. Let them discover that action doesn't have to "match" the words.

Action as Proposal

I believe and hope to prove to my classes that all reality created onstage is physical and active. If you just say that something is true, it doesn't necessarily make it true. If you play something, it is instantly true and undeniable. All creation of improvised material comes from the interplay of two forces—proposal and justification—with the principle of agreement as law. Work to encourage your improvisers to work from action proposals instead of just verbal. This will lift the level of physical play and result in more creative ideas.

Action Leads. Have one player in the center space generate actions of all sorts, random or obvious, to which one or more outside players provide creative verbal/sonic justifications. Don't let the justifications turn into a story. Let it be a cascade of all the possible explanations of the player's action and intentions. Complicate the exercise by inviting two players to play together in the center.

Reporter. One player "reports" on the freely generated actions of a group of players. Add style to the reporter: sports commentary, war journalist, opera synopsis. Don't let the players' action follow the reporter!

Outside Switch. Play Switch (also known as Freeze) with the justification of the action coming from the players not onstage. Two players begin action from the freeze and instead of them talking the scene to life, someone from the outside provides the justification and then calls "Freeze!" to tag one out and join. Complicate the exercise by playing in a group of three, two players and one outside at all times.

Physical Nonsense Initiation. One player initiates the scene with a "nonsense" action that the other player (or players) joins and justifies somehow. The action must be specific and continuous yet nothing we know of yet. Don't let the scene be "about" the action itself.

Turn Off the Talk

When I started directing Touring Company archive material, Sheldon Patinkin advised, "Watch the videos." Most Second City scenes live in the action, not the words on the page. I remember one in particular called "Divorce" from the show *Upstage, Downstage* (1977), which reads as a touching let's-get-back-together scene for father, mother, and child. Not that funny a read. On the video, however, the audience is in stitches. Steve Kampmann, playing the child, is bouncing off the walls with hyperactive energy, threatening everything in his path. You have to *do* things to improvise, not say things.

Spolin engineered countless preverbal and nonverbal exercises to attack the problem of losing physical play in improvisation through talk. Turn off the words if the scene is dying. Get your players used to your sidecoaching them to switch to gibberish and back. It clarifies what's going on or what's not. And then the improvisers will have to *do something.* Many improvisers think of gibberish as a beginning exercise, but it is hilarious and fun at any level. In the scene "Diplomat" from *Paradigm Lost* (1996), Rachel Dratch and Kevin Dorff bring down the house with gibberish. Here are some great ways to turn off talk and turn on physical action choices:

Only Two. In this simple structure that I use, all the players stand in a line at the back of the space. The rule is that only two players are allowed onstage at a time, yet always two. The two onstage create any action without speech. As one or more enter, those onstage must exit so that no more than two remain onstage at a time. The action should never die onstage yet develop. Play it fast with lots of exits and entrances. Play it ascending style—with only three, only four, and so on—until only one is offstage at a time. This is very challenging to keep unified.

Silent Switch (Freeze). Same form, no talking. You will find the same energy, hilarious changes in situation, as well as more attention paid to creative physical positions instead of "clever" ideas.

Silent Two-Scenes. Same form, no talking. Have the scenes in the same Where. Can the two simultaneous scenes trade focus just by level of action?

Silent Scene Tag. Same form, no talking, and an extension of Silent Two-Scenes. Have the players create weaving scenes that continue after edits. This is an excellent way to develop character and relationship through physical action as opposed to talk.

Because the action is silent doesn't mean players need to indicate or mime to clarify what's going on. Some will be tempted to "sign" the action. They should just listen, agree, and do. A joke that needs explaining isn't a joke.

Exercising Physical Control

By removing or assigning some aspect of the players' control of the physical, you can elicit great creative solutions to the problem. Here are some exercise ideas.

External Tilt. An outside caller calls "Tilt!" at key points where an immediate physical reaction/event/accident must happen and be justified into the scene.

Three Feet Only. Without furniture, play a scene where two actors have only three feet on the floor at any time during the whole scene. Try it with only two feet.

Continuous Activity Scene. Don't let the players drop a strong physical activity of the scene (yet not let it be the only content or destroy the flow of the scene!). There are infinite ideas: holding up a boulder, cleaning an elephant, wrestling, drumming, driving (very hard to do and stay believable).

VCR. An outside caller changes the pace of the scene onstage through VCR controls: fast-forward, rewind, stop, freeze-frame, frame by frame, slo-mo, and so on.

Rewind with Physical Heightening. Play a simple scene through several beats. Stop and have the scene reimprovised with amplified physical choices. Replay again with even greater choices.

Puppeteer. Each actor has a puppeteer creating their physical choices for them. The physical equivalent of the gibberish translation exercise Dubbing.

Blind Scene. One player is blindfolded, but not blind in the scene. Try it with both players blindfolded at your own risk.

Combat Sequence. Let the players improvise with only this caveat: at some point in this scene there will be a fight. (Emphasize safety and the use of illusion here.)

Dance Number/Chase Sequence. Similar to Combat Sequence. Let the players improvise with only this caveat: at some point in this scene there will be a dance number. Or the same with a chase sequence.

Music Videos. Have the group bring cuts of music, exchange them, and without rehearsal or listening ahead, the group generates a music video. (Music and sound are excellent leaders of action.)

I remind improvisers that improv is a full-body activity. Improv is an exercise of muscle, spirit, *and* mind. To me, studying martial arts, circus arts, commedia, sport, dance, contact improvisation, and so on are as important for a Second City improviser as reading the newspaper or keeping up with comedy. What suspends and entertains an audience is what's going on in the scene, not just what's said. The greater the level of physical action, the more exciting Second City work becomes. In the same way, improvisers know that the more dedicated physically they are to the moment, the more exciting and easy it is to play.

—*Dexter Bullard*

AN IMPROVISATIONAL ALMANAC: PART TWO

Take responsibility for your actions. You are not always responsible for your character's words onstage.

⋄ ⋄ ⋄

Wear your character as lightly as you would a hat; be ready to tip it to reveal yourself.

⋄ ⋄ ⋄

Play against clichés. Blacks, gays, Hispanics, and so on, if played as clichés, will be less of a character and more of a caricature, which is not what we are really after.

⋄ ⋄ ⋄

Play the game by the rules to the best of your ability.

⋄ ⋄ ⋄

A space can be anything you want it to be and can have anything you want to have in it. Once something is there, though, it is there.

⋄ ⋄ ⋄

Recognize the space. Own it. Use it. Make it yours. Adapt, adopt, and improve it by making discoveries that help define it even more.

⋄ ⋄ ⋄

Show, don't tell. Trust that the audience will see and they will respect you even more.

⋄ ⋄ ⋄

Be prepared for anything, like a Boy Scout.

⋄ ⋄ ⋄

Straight actors in plays have to trust their lines and the play. Improvisers have to trust the moment and the other actors in the moment. This trust will be reflected in the reality of the moment.

❧ ❧ ❧

Accept what your partner does or says as a gift, not as a challenge.

❧ ❧ ❧

Accept the other players' reality.

❧ ❧ ❧

Do not ask questions if you can avoid it. Turn the question around and make a statement out of it. Questions put the responsibility on your partners.

❧ ❧ ❧

Make assumptions but don't script write. You have only what you have discovered in the improv. Again, try to stay out of your head and in the space. Know each other. Avoid introductions by sharing an assumed past.

❧ ❧ ❧

Keep the action onstage. Don't story tell or plan for the future. Try not to bring up the past. Try not to focus on people or animals that aren't there. It's very difficult to have a scene on what is not there in the now.

❧ ❧ ❧

One should always know what the audience knows or has just learned. Playing against this will lead to denial.

❧ ❧ ❧

Don't let the little details go. By being ecological one can create the whole. Those little details are all you have to build the bigger things out of. Remember the details.

❧ ❧ ❧

When cocharacters play together in a scene, the time to have known each other is between a couple of weeks and many, many years. The ability to discover things about each other over many years can't be reproduced onstage, yet the comfort of knowing each other and those discovery results can come across in the comfort of the moment.

❧ ❧ ❧

Play the realities as if you are living them for the first time—yet every discovery must be made freshly, in a unique way.

⟿ ⟿ ⟿

Think of all your possibilities or think of all the availabilities.

⟿ ⟿ ⟿

End a scene after a new element has been added or a new discovery made. Also, if you are entering a scene, enter knowing that you are either ending it or adding information to help further it. Try not to prolong the agony of a scene that is slowly dying, but infuse it with the momentum it needs to end on a positive note.

⟿ ⟿ ⟿

Every character ever written, played, or made is inside you. Release them as necessary.

⟿ ⟿ ⟿

Rather than focusing your energy on what you are going to say, focus on the point of view of the character's or the group's activity.

⟿ ⟿ ⟿

Think of the environment as a multidimensional Where of which the audience is a part. The environment also contains an outside, or beyond, and an inside; focus in and focus out.

⟿ ⟿ ⟿

One can do anything onstage. If one does it honestly it is believable. This enables us to travel in time.

CHAPTER THREE: THE PERFORMER INSIDE THE SCENE

A Few Thoughts on Improvisation

INSTRUCTOR: Improvisation, improvisation, improvisation! How many
 times have we heard that word?

STUDENT: Well, that's three times now.

Funny joke, eh? I'll answer for you. Yes, quite a funny joke, and fitting for the topic. I first heard it on a Second City stage many years ago. Even before I ever worked there. My point is that Second City improv is not about jokes, but it never hurts to go into battle with a few funny bullets in your gun.

I still work occasionally with improv groups and I'm overwhelmed by the popularity of improv and also by how remarkably good so many improv performers are. There are improvisational workshops and shows everywhere: games, styles, warm-ups.

My first impression of Second City was watching Alan Arkin, Severn Darden, Howard Alk, and Andrew Duncan, a montage of bearded science and philosophy major types, and actresses like Barbara Harris, exotic and complex. They had studied under Paul Sills and Viola Spolin. Although I was not part of that, I believe the idea was to create a scene that was a social comment; it could go on forever (never too long for me), and if there were no jokes, all the better.

When I was asked to join the company (there was no touring company or farm system then) I was petrified. What did I know about Kierkegaard or Immanuel Kant? I had also never improvised. The thought scared me. But after a puzzlingly satisfying audition, I was like the actor who says, "Of course, I can ride a horse." When I arrived, along with Robert Klein, a charming actress named Judy Graubart, and a fellow who is now a successful sportswear salesman in New York, we were not under the direction of Paul Sills. Our director was a young gentleman who was not that much senior to us in Second City experience. His name was Sheldon Patinkin. And Sheldon gave us something many other directors could never provide. He gave us a gentle guidance and a chance to learn on our feet. The only rules I remember were to never negate what another actor has said, and don't go for a joke. He would also occasionally explain to us that what we thought was new and hilarious had just recently been done by Paul Sand or Mina Kolb. The men wore suits onstage. One night in an improv an actor said, "Shit." We were in the dressing room less than a minute when we heard Sheldon's footsteps charging down the hall. "Never, ever use that word onstage again!" he warned. Well, times have changed. But in essence he was right. Street language can be very effective if used right (like nudity), but funny, bright, and clean is unbeatable. It's tougher, but unbeatable. My first improv scene onstage involved a penguin on a subway platform. I watched from the wings, wishing the actors onstage luck. Someone said to me, "Go on out as a cop!" and gave me a push. I had nothing. But from somewhere words came and the scene went great. (Actually, probably just okay, but in my memory it was great.) The next night, full of my talent, I watched an improv where two actors argued about whether their friend died of a heart attack or was hit by a truck. What a joke I thought of! I waltzed onstage and when the time was right, said, "You'd have a heart attack too if you were hit by a truck." Pretty nice laugh. But then I had nowhere to go. So much for jokes. Oh yes, Sheldon also warned about going on with an extreme character or quirk, because if it didn't work you were stuck with it.

Several years later I was asked to teach an improv class to college students at the Circle in the Square theater in New York City for two months. Since the salary equaled my rent, I said yes. But I still felt insecure about teaching. However, I plowed ahead with my method, which I still think is good. First I had them pair up and do the Mirror exercise. It's one exercise I endorse, because it forces you to concentrate on your partner. Then I had them practice sense memory. I had them pass around an imaginary basketball. I learned something surprising. Three out of four did it properly. The rest closed their hands together, no matter how many times I corrected them. It was then that I thought, I don't think you can teach improv like you can teach piano or golf. There will always be the actor who will take me out of a scene by getting out of a car and walking through the engine to cross the stage. Also, I will forever admire the actor who holds an imaginary drink and then carefully sets it down before moving on. (Doing so even after the blackout borders on genius, but is not a necessity.) So, what to do with my eager students? I got them up in pairs and gave them situations, opening lines, characters, and places. If they came to learn improv, I might as well let them improv. If they'd come to learn baseball, I would have brought out bats and balls.

It was fun for the students and it's still the best way to learn, as far as I'm concerned. Get up and improvise. And do it with the best improvisers you can find. Hopefully, at first, you'll be the worst in the group. But you will rise. If you work with weak improvisers you'll end up either showing off, for which everyone will dislike you, or holding back, for fear of throwing your partners. Conversely, it's a great learning tool to watch bad improv, just like watching bad acting. You'll say, "Oh no, that's something I might do. I must remember never to do that." You'll make your own list of rules.

Here's another thing I learned. When I was a Second City member, alumni would come back and we'd ask them to join in the set. I could never understand when they'd say no. But now when I go back I feel the same way. Lack of constant practice opens up that little door in your head that says, "Is what I'm about to say going to sound foolish?" It's the biggest block to creativity. So stand up and do it. Listen to your partners. Don't fish for jokes. Be well read and aware of what's going on in the news. Also pain! Pain helps. Show me a good improviser and he's had pain in his life. Pain makes for good comedy and good country songs. Also have opinions. The whole point of comedy is to point out hypocrisy, pretension, and mendacity. As Freud once said . . . well, what did Freud say? He said, "Sometimes a cigar is just a cigar." I know it has nothing to do with this subject, but people are always impressed when you can quote a philosopher . . . and don't you forget it.

—*Fred Willard*

Finding the Funny

It's the question that comes up so often in improvisation classes: "All this stuff about environment and supporting my partner is fine, but how do I get to be funny?" Fred Willard, from his early work with Second City through Fernwood 2Night *and most recently in movies like* Waiting for Guffman *and* Best in Show, *has proven to be one of the most consistently funny of the many brilliantly hysterical Second City alumni. It seems our students look at the impressive list of comedians who have graced our various stages and expect that somewhere in our theater exists the secret to making an audience laugh. When it comes up in my own classes, I often respond with an answer similar to one of Fred's: comedy is connected to pain. Andrew Currie, who teaches at the Toronto Training Center and performed on the Toronto Mainstage from 1993 to 1996, has a few other excellent answers.*

If you haven't seen it for yourself, you probably know the cliché. A hack stand-up comic sets himself up for his best impersonation:

" . . . But ya know what would be *really* crazy, folks? What if Jack Nicholson was captain of the *Enterprise*? I think it would go a little something like this. . . ."

Similar material echoed through the halls of clubs across the continent during the stand-up boom of the late 1980s. These days you'll hopefully only hear it on reruns of *The Simpsons*, and with good reason—for the purposes of Second City–style improvisation, it's dead wrong. "Wouldn't it be funny if . . . ?" concepts have no place in our work, and I'll show you why.

One of the biggest challenges any Second City instructor faces with new students is trying to get them to stop making up stuff. Just like all the civilians who watch *Whose Line* on TV, improv newbies tend to look at the craft as a vehicle for demonstrating how clever they are. I know, because I used to think that way myself. In the spring of 1993, Sheldon Patinkin came up from Chicago to workshop the Toronto Touring Company. His assessment of my particular skill set: "You rely too much on your wit." No problem, I thought; I could do worse than to be a funny, clever guy. As if reading my mind, he added: "And when that wit runs out, what else have you got?"

Improv secret 1: you don't have to find the funny; the funny will find you. All you have to do is play the scene.

As legend has it, when someone handed jazz musician John Coltrane a transcription of one of his very own sax solos, he couldn't play it. Why? Because, he apparently said, "it's too hard." Similar stories run in Second City circles, and I've been fortunate enough to have the same experience on-stage myself. If someone were to ask me afterward how I could ever come up with whatever it was I had come up with, I could only shrug and say, "Sorry, I don't remember."

To dismiss me as an aloof prick would be only half right. The more important truth is that on this particular occasion I was *playing the scene.* If you set up a proper exposition with a strong Who, What, Where and stay true to your character, then as the scene unfolds the audience will be with you every step of the way, no matter how strange things get. Even better, that same plot progression will be easy for you and your scene partners, since it will make perfect sense to your characters!

To suddenly jump from plot point B to plot point X would be what we call a non sequitur, as in this example:

"Honey, we have to talk...."
"Let's go to Mars!"

If, however, your audience sees how a trip to the red planet can ultimately make sense in the reality you've created, then by all means blast off! You've earned yourselves a pair of first-class tickets....

Improv secret 2: replace "Wouldn't it be funny if ...?" with "Isn't it funny that...?"

One of the many things that laughter is is the sound of the audience congratulating itself, maybe because they've understood the logic that has brought a lovers' quarrel to an Martian expedition, or perhaps because a scene touches on some experience that they themselves have had. Within the concept of shared experience is a veritable comedy gold mine; it will lead you on the path to understanding that biggest of big words, *satire.*

When I hired people [for the Compass Players] . . . I was going on something you could not measure, which was a sense of their insight into what was happening in society and their ability to play a whole bunch of parts. . . . [That] included whatever characters Barbara Harris had been studying for years. And she was studying her mother for years. And Elaine May had also been studying under *her* mother for years. They could do their mothers brilliantly. And Elaine May had also been studying Hollywood starlets, and she knew about uptight secretaries. And Severn Darden had been studying German professors for years. He did them for days at the Compass.

—*David Shepard*

I confess that I didn't really figure out satire until after I had left the Toronto Mainstage, mostly because I was in a younger cast performing for a mostly older audience. It was often that I didn't fully appreciate the manner in which my directors would help shape the scenes I was in. I was dumbfounded when something that I thought was funny and insightful all along only began to resonate with an audience after the director had tweaked it. I realize now that what my brilliant directors had done was tap into experiences that they and our audience had shared. Satire doesn't have to be about politics; it can be found by the bucketful in something as simple as a family dinner. And while not too many of us have firsthand experience with being president of the United States, everyone has some experience with family politics. When I saw fellow Second City alum Nia Vardalos's hit movie *My Big Fat Greek Wedding*, the biggest laugh from the audience came from this single line of dialogue: "So your family is crazy. . . . Whose *isn't?*" This is but one example of the untapped wealth of shared experience available to you as a writer, director, actor, or improviser.

So there it is, the only thing you'll have to find. And if you play it right, the funny will be there too!

—*Andrew Currie*

How Do You Create Characters? or "I Do This Hilarious Guy Who Has a Funny Hat"

In The Second City Training Center, Level 2 of the Conservatory Program is "Character." When I went through the program, Mick Napier was my brilliant and inspiring Level 2 instructor. The first day of class, he asked us to raise our hands if we found it hard to play characters. Nearly every hand in the class, mine included, went up.

From the early days of Second City's precursor the Compass Players, with performers like Elaine May and Alan Arkin, to the entire cast of SCTV, our history of brilliant character actors/improvisers is an intimidating one to live up to. But Mick taught my class that once we shed the burden of historical precedent, character work set us free. Playing a character can make improvising infinitely easier. Often I find that the character will know what to say when I am paralyzed and blocked.

Taking those first steps to finding the character are often the hardest. Dave Razowsky, who offers the first of our essays on character, is the artistic director of The Second City Los Angeles and alum of the Chicago stages, where he was one of the character actors we all wanted to emulate.

Contrary to what one might think, a hat or a wig shop isn't the place to find your characters. Nor is Dr. O'Haja's Yuk Emporium. The same doesn't go for your Uncle Mort's closet. Nuh-uh. Working on character begins just where you might think (if you'd been thinking)—in your own limber and welcoming body parts.

Of course you can accessorize the characters at the preceding locations once you've built 'em, but let's not get ahead of ourselves. The creation of that character requires the actor to take a look in the mirror and to take a walk around his body. Remember that a "real character" goes beyond a sight gag or a quick joke.[1] A real character is one that an audience can relate to, one that is intelligent and has a heart, a person we can look at and see ourselves in or someone we know. A character has a soul and transcends caricature. And just in terms of working at The Second City, a real character with real needs and real emotions is easier to improvise with than one who deals with the lowest common denominator or goes for the easy laugh. The more real we can make our characters, the easier it is to discover what the scene is about and create smart, funny, and courageous work.

In other words, it ain't easy to create a character, but don't let that scare you.

Contrary to popular belief, character creation does not begin at any

---

1. I don't mean to imply that the characters we see on late-night network weekend programming aren't "real characters." The term "real characters" is just the definition I'll use for this essay solely for the purpose of clarity, understanding, and honesty. No one has ever said that a character based on a funny pair of prosthetic teeth or a prosthetic chin whose only trait seems to be that he's (sing it!) "Jimmy . . . the Guy Who Can't Use Verbs" isn't a real character. I know plenty of people who can't use verbs, and whenever I see late-night network weekend programming actors portraying them on late-night network weekend programming I say to myself, "Hey, that's just like my friend Bob who can't use verbs. Those guys nailed it!" But what say we get out of this footnote and back to the point(s).

Additional Character Exercises

CHARACTER DESCRIPTION: *To Play.* Players face each other. Player A describes player B's character completely, beginning with what she is wearing on her feet, finishing with details such as name and age. As player B is being described she physically adjusts, "taking on" as many of the details of the character provided as she can. Player B then describes player A. The characters described need not correspond in any way with the physicality of the performer. They can be taller, fatter, balder, younger, whatever you choose. Descriptions should keep incongruities to a minimum—the idea here is to create an actual human being, not to pimp your partner into having to justify a set of bizarre details.

Based on these characters, the two players set up a simple Who, What, Where and play a scene. Just as in Environment Description, the details should inform the scene but not become the focus of the scene. In other words, don't talk about it; just respond to it.

Variations. (1) Players do the descriptions privately and then do the scene for the rest of the group. See how much of the original physicality the audience can guess from watching behavior in the scene. (2) Try this exercise along with Environment Description; start by fully describing the environment and then create characters who belong there. You can also use the two exercises together to create "style" scenes—describe environment and characters from a specific film or theatrical genre—say film noir or western—and see what happens when you play within that physical space.

THREE SCENES: This is primarily a classroom or rehearsal exercise designed to develop three-dimensional characters; however, if you pretty it up a bit, it makes a nice scenic performance piece.

To Play. One actor plays the same character in three scenes with three different actors. Either player can initiate the first scene but the entering players should initiate the next two. Entering players should look for ways to explore a new facet of the existing character while supporting the creation that already exists. Editing may be done either externally or by players entering from a back line.

HYPERTEXT: This game was created by a Level 3 class I taught at Second City, out of a discussion about how to get the actual experience of being online onto a stage (as opposed to miming keyboards and mice). It works best with six or more players and is one of the few performance games that seem to work better the more people you have playing. It works equally well as a classroom exercise or a semi-long-form performance game. If you do it in performance, create a designated caller or rotate individuals out after they have been primary in a scene.

To Play. Start with a location in which a bunch of people might gather. Everyone onstage becomes someone (or some-

store or resale shop or at any of the many "funny voice workshops."[2] Character work begins with the body of the actor, and through the body of the actor directly comes the point of view of the character. For lack of a better word, the actor must begin by "isolating" different parts of her body and seeing how that inspires the creation of the character. This physical isolation leads to amazing discoveries in terms of character development. Through physical work the characters look and feel more organic, more real, more like people we know. Plus, at the core of all Second City scenes is the relationship. The truer we can portray characters, the more based in reality our work will be.

Creating characters through body isolation starts with finding your personal neutral zone. I know it sounds a little, well, queer, but your neutral zone is the way you walk, the way you hold your shoulders, where your head rests on your neck, with what part of your body you lead. Once you've defined your neutral zone, walk around and, starting with your feet, overemphasize your walk, leading with your feet. Play with walking pigeon-toed, feet splayed out, a heavy step, a light step. Pay particular attention to how those physical transformations make you feel, mentally and emotionally. This emotional core is the root of your character. Attaining that emotion through the character's physical quirks leads to wonderful discoveries. Ask yourself (either aloud or in the windmill of your mind), who would walk this way? How old are they? What do they do for a living? What was the highest degree they received at school?[3] Now give the character a name and, finally, see what kind of voice comes out of this character you've created. See how something as simple as changing the way a person walks can affect the way you make her sound.

As you move about the space, taking the time to isolate your knees, pelvis, stomach, chest, and head, ask yourself those same questions. (Be sure to go back to your neutral zone before moving on to the next body area.) To discover a character, we must work from the physical *first*. As you

---

2. Many of these so-called workshops are taught by hacks or people who are just trying to cash in on their own speech impediments. Make sure a bonded insured "Funny Voice Instructor" helms any funny voice workshop you take.

3. Many of these are questions asked at a job interview. Don't let that scare you.

go on you'll discover that the success of creating your characters isn't based on costumes or props, but rather on the way you feel when walking within the confines of a body that is isolating certain physical traits.

Because we don't have the luxury to do these exercises each time before we go onstage we need to get into the habit of checking in with our physical selves the moment we hit the stage. This requires us to be aware of how we step onto that stage, where our arms are, and how we carry ourselves, and to then let those aspects create our character for us. If I walk onstage with a heavy step, I will make that a part of my character and see where that takes him. If I should have one hand in my pocket and the other holding on to my jacket, I'll let that inform my character. Inherent in this approach is a bit of trust, a touch of the Zen, and a whole lot of the "dare to fail" attitude.

But isn't that what all the work is about?

—Dave Razowsky

Playing at the Top of Your Intelligence

It's one of the great improv truths, repeated to countless students by countless teachers of improvisation. When you improvise you should play at the top of your intelligence.

For some reason, many improvisers hear this and understand it as, "You must constantly display any knowledge you possess to the audience." Nothing could be further from the truth. Playing at the top of your intelligence is not about constantly quoting Shakespeare or using the Pythagorean theorem in conversation. It is this simple—everything you see and perceive while you are onstage, your character sees and perceives as well. If you recognize that the other characters have hidden motives, then your character must notice those motives as well. Because your character is a different person than you are, she will filter that information differently and this will affect her subsequent actions. You may be playing a child, a retarded person, or a Nobel Prize–winning physicist; each of those characters will interpret the same information differently and respond differently as a result of that interpretation.

And just because you are playing at the top of your intelligence does

thing) in that location. Two or three players take focus and begin a scene; the rest of the players stay in the background. The caller freezes the action and instructs the audience that they are viewing a page on the Web; every person is highlighted, so who would they like to "click on" and see more of? The person who is clicked on steps forward *in the character he has been playing in the background of the scene* and introduces himself in character. He then takes the action to a new location and becomes primary in a new scene. Everyone else becomes a new character in that new location, and one or two players take focus and join in the scene.

The idea here is to invest as fully as possible in your background character while not pulling focus from the scene in progress. If you elect to be an inanimate object or an animal, be sure to invest just as strongly in an inner life because chances are very good that you will be chosen, and you will need to star in a new scene and still portray the animal or object.

not mean that your character will behave intelligently or in his own best interest. One of my favorite improvisers is Neil Flynn, who performed on our ETC stage before moving to California, where he now appears on the NBC sitcom *Scrubs*. During an improvised scene, Neil will often call out what is going on: "You're messing with my head. I know this will all end badly but I'm going to go along with you on this because I really want you to like me." Audiences love this; they are smart enough to have seen what was going on and now they know that the actors and characters know too. The scene acquires depth and richness because the characters are aware of their actions and their potential fate.

As long as you play at the top of your intelligence, your characters' behavior will be grounded in truth. Occasionally this truth will end up being a flash of intellectual insight—"This moment is just like Kafka's *Metamorphosis.*" If and when that happens, you will get a laugh and it will be laughter of recognition, based on the fact that the audience knows that you are perceiving something true and responding to it and not just showing off your education.

Character: Playing with Intelligence and Heart

Nick Johne, who teaches in our Toronto Training Center and performed in the Canadian Mainstage cast with Andrew Currie, now takes this idea of playing to the top of your intelligence even further into the idea of playing at the top of the character's intelligence.

Often, when teaching a workshop in character, I find myself coaching the actors, over and over, to play their characters to the top of their intelligence. But it wasn't until just recently that I actually sat down and thought about what that phrase actually means.

Playing to the top of the character's intelligence . . . hmm. Here's the gist of it. When improvising, one must come up with unique, believable, three-dimensional characters in the blink of an eye. If the scene requires a construction worker, go in and be a construction worker. If the scene requires a priest, get in there and be a priest.

Let's say we're in a class and we're doing the scene that requires a construction worker. We start the scene and what we usually get is a scene where the construction worker is your garden variety stereotypical Italian, complete with hairy chest, bad accent, and bad attitude. You know, a stereotype! A cartoon version of the construction worker, not a character.

I let this scene continue (unless of course some of the choices made are horrible, dangerous, or racist) and we laugh and applaud. Then, out come some of my questions. I ask the class, "Was the construction worker believable? Have we seen construction workers like this? Do they behave this way and do they all speak with the same accent as, say, Chico Marx?"

I usually get a whole slew of answers, most of them "No," and we inevitably conclude together that the construction worker need not be played as a stereotype. Of course then the floodgates open and I get a whole slew of questions thrown right back at me. Questions like, "How do we play a construction worker without going for the stereotype?" and "Is it wrong to play an Italian construction worker?"

My short answer to these and other questions is that you can play anything you want as long as you play it to the top of yours and the character's intelligence. By this, I mean make smart, well informed, heartfelt choices for the character.

Again, let's take a look at our construction worker. Let's give him an age. Say, he's about twenty-five years old. Let's make him a first- or second-generation child of immigrants so that he doesn't speak with your cartoon version Italian accent. Maybe (and at this point we'll give him a name) Joe has some postsecondary education in business or perhaps even something as esoteric as philosophy. Joe loves his parents very much and is respectful of his mother. Given all that, what does Joe look like? How does he behave now, as he sits on a steel girder somewhere up on the twenty-third floor of the new skyscraper being built downtown? What does he talk about to his coworkers and friends?

You can see that by making some quick, smart choices, one can transform the portrayal of the construction worker from the ethnic stereotype into something that is rich and full blown.

Simple, yes? Not quite.

Here comes the hard part. I mentioned earlier that in order to play a character at the top of one's intelligence, one also has to make some heartfelt choices. Ah yes, the heart, that ineffable part of everyone's performance without which acting or improvising just becomes an intellectual exercise.

If you play to the highest level of your own intelligence and assume the audience is at least as intelligent as you are, you will find your audience. If you do anything else, they sense it and they don't like you for it. The smart ones. The dumb ones you don't care about.

—*Bernie Sahlins*

Three Kinds of Character

There are three general types of characters that we use on a Second City stage. The first is a stage manifestation of yourself. This is the character you use for introductions and calling performance games. Second is the character who is defined by a simple narrow comic perspective: not a cliché or a cartoon but someone who views the world through a specific filter—the hardware salesman who sees nuts and bolts wherever he goes, the sports fan whose world is defined by the misfortunes of his chosen team. These characters are useful for group scenes or for performance games such as Panel of Experts or Poet's Corner.

The third is more fully three dimensional. These types of characters may also have a strong comic perspective but over time they display more facets and contradictions. These characters almost develop a life of their own, showing up in multiple scenes and improvisations, growing and changing as they do so. These are the characters that serve us best in classic behavior or relationship scenes.

I once had an acting teacher who told me that the heart never lies. Your brain may tell you little white lies, your intellect may pull the wool over your eyes, but your heart will never lead you astray. That's all well and fine but what does this acting from the heart thing exactly mean?

Well, let's take a look at our friend the construction worker once again. What status does he have? Does he make eye contact with his coworkers or does he avoid it? Whom does he like? Whom is he afraid of? Maybe Joe has a limp or some other physical quirk. Or perhaps there's something that he's particularly proud of.

Again these are choices that can be made quickly and on the fly, turning a potential cartoon into something more compelling. At the root of these choices is how the actor actually feels about the character. I think that ultimately the actor has to like the character, even though the character itself might be totally unsympathetic.

Here's a quick example. I was once teaching a class and we were doing Goon River, which for me is not only a great narrative game but also a good character game, in that we have four or five characters telling their life stories in a fairly controlled forum. One of the actors made the choice to play a virulent bigot. The character was horrible; things that were spewing out of his mouth were utterly reprehensible and truly hateful. It was one of the most compelling things I'd ever seen improvised. Why? Because, despite the rather risky choices made, the choices were all honest and from the guy's heart, so that what we saw wasn't the idea of a racist, but the embodiment of one. It was as if a mirror had been held up and the actor had said, "See, there are monsters out there and this is what they're like!"

The improviser was using his heart to access some very dark places. Sure it was scary, but because he worked with his heart the portrayal had the stench of truth about it. Oddly none of the other students cringed while watching this rather "challenging" performance and all agreed that it was a truthful portrayal. It worked because of the force of recognition; in a less honest situation this portrayal would have been truly offensive on so many levels.

Now I'm not sure whether this acting from the heart can be taught, but I do think that people can be pointed in the general direction. One way I feel that can be done is to concentrate on the physical component of the character. It's been my experience that if you start working on the body, the heart will soon follow. If you get someone working on physicality—any kind of physicality, be it a nervous tic, a body posture, or whatever—it's a sure way to short-circuit the intellect and to allow the actor's heart to take over.

But what exactly do I mean by the "heart"? For me it's a whole bunch of things. It's gaining access to your own instinct about a given situation. It's playing the characters truthfully. But more important, it boils down to accessing that part of yourself where your own inner truths lie. If this makes any sense, it's not what you wear but what you bring to the dance, or the scene, that's important.

One of the things I tell my students is that in improv, there's no such thing as a bad choice; there are only good choices and better choices. Playing characters to the top of their intelligence and from the heart will allow you to make the best choices possible.

And if you play to the top, the choices are limitless.

GOON RIVER: *Number of Players.* Five, each sitting in a chair with their eyes closed

To Play. The basic premise of Goon River is that the five people doing the exercise are the dead inhabitants of a small town and are recounting their lives and the events leading up to their deaths. It's based on Edgar Lee Masters's *Spoon River Anthology.* The exercise itself can be broken up into three parts. In the first part the characters introduce who they are and what their job or significance is in the town of Goon River. After they each have done that, in the second part they describe one relationship with one of the already established characters. In the third part, the characters recount the events leading up to their deaths. As said, this is done with eyes closed, so there is no particular order. The only stipulation is that the exercise is done in the three steps described here. It works the narrative muscle; all the threads of the story should somehow interrelate. It works the character muscle, as in this case character often drives the narrative forward. And because this is done with eyes closed, it also works that old listening muscle, forcing you to have big ears.

—*Nick Johne*

In the Beginning . . . Making Initiations

I think one of the most difficult things to do as an improviser is to walk the line between making strong choices and surrendering your better idea to the other choices made necessary by the scene. As a performer, Susan Messing has always been the queen of the brave and inspired choice, whether improvising with the Annoyance Theater (where she was in the original cast of the long-running Coed Prison Sluts*) or during her stint on The Second City Chicago Mainstage. As a teacher, she is like a ball of pure energy, simultaneously creating a safe space for her students while she asks them to perform what feels to be nearly impossible.*

It's the top of the scene. My partner looks at me expectantly, waiting for a line of dialogue to pop out of my mouth. I stare blankly back. For a second, I remember that weird kid in kindergarten whose mom always had to bring him a new change of clothes because he pooped himself. When that moment has passed, my scene partner is still staring at me. I have no idea what to do or say. By this point, I might be considering why I thought it would be "fun" to even consider improvising in the first place. Welcome to hell.

Or perhaps I have a *fantastic* idea for a scene that I am *sure* will be really, *really* funny. Maybe I got high in my tub last night and worked out all the important moments, complete with the characters' backstories. I even had the opportunity to try it out at the office with the guy in the cubby next to me and it *killed.* I open my mouth to begin my surefire *brilliance* and my partner beats me to the chase. "Dr. Miller," he says, "I started an IV with D5W." I am noticeably confused and subsequently pissed off. *My* scene *clearly* was meant to occur in the hot tub at the Caesar's Resort in the Poconos. I was even (before my partner so rudely inflicted *his* idea on me) going to give some really funny business to my partner, letting him burn his balls to a pulp. And now that fucker has ruined everything, *everything,* do you hear me? And yes, welcome to hell.

I used to be an improviser who blamed others when I didn't have fun onstage. I'd wail, "Why does he *always* decide what the scene is?" if my partner initiated or "Why doesn't he follow *my* ideas? I started it!" I was always a victim of my scene, constantly profoundly disappointed that my partner couldn't read my mind . . . until I figured out some basic major truths. If I *don't* have fun, it's *my own damn fault* and the *only* thing I own in a scene is *me.* Everything else is to be discovered by my scene partner and myself. After all, it's *improv.*

Even the most experienced improvisers have "off" days and "shit" scenes. But through the years I have noticed certain tactics employed to "up" their success quotient . . . and it all takes place in the first three seconds of the scene. My always teacher, Mick Napier, said that the audience knows who you are in the first three seconds of the scene, even if you didn't make a *deliberate* choice. Another teacher, Rebecca Sohn, added a very wise clarification: the choices you make at the top of the scene are your *promise* to the audience as to who you're going to be, and it is your responsibility to remember and honor your choices.

At the top of the scene, take care of yourself. Since your body is all you own, if you want to explore another character, you might lead with a different part of your spine and see where it takes you. As Mick would say, "Do something. *Anything.*" It doesn't matter who speaks first because an initiation does not determine the outcome of the scene. An initiation is only the *beginning.* Everything else is to be discovered by you and your partner as you build the scene together.

Sometimes people will initiate with plot. "Here is our problem and our tree fort is burning while we're here in Idaho and I hate you because of that thing you always do and let me show you how to do this right and what are you doing blah blah blah." Nothing particularly wrong with it, but wouldn't you rather *discover* what your scene is rather than spewing some convoluted idea that you won't even remember in a minute? Take your time. Go line by line. Add to the picture that already exists. How about enjoying your journey instead of shooting your left-brain wad? Besides, scenes are about relationships between human beings, not about plot or even about (dare I say when mentioning comedy?) "funny."

When I am patient, recommit to my initiations, and listen to my partner, the plot and the funny naturally emerge, and then by the end of the scene I am able to delight in the "How did we get from this initiation to *here?*" feeling with my partner. No matter what, I've enjoyed the journey

Crossing the Line and Going Blue

I have a very nostalgic slant toward Second City. My feeling is when someone comes here and looks at all the pictures on the walls of [famous alumni], they shouldn't sit in the audience and feel as if they've been violated. I feel like I need to protect that. I feel like I want them to have a good time, and I want the place to live up to its tradition and all of the people that they know came from here. At the same time, I don't want them to get away scot-free. I want them to be a little challenged. I want them to be a little offended and I trust that I can protect that. [In *Second City 4.0*] there is a line where Rich Talarico is singing a song and he says, "Sucking dick for booze"; I learned from *Groundhog Day* that if I had him repeat that, I would contextually protect that moment. It did, for a while. Then the show shaped itself in different ways where the line was sticking out like a sore thumb for me. So I brought another little stylistic choice where these two characters march upstage into the sunset. Then it felt good. I felt as if I got away with it. I felt as if the audience could accept it; I felt okay. I don't like to pander to the audiences here but I also don't like to offend them. I have a real strong stand on that too. If offending the audience is your thing, why not have the lights come up and just say, "Fuck you, fuck you, fuck you," until they leave.

—*Mick Napier*

There is a theory about comedy that what comedians and actors do is portray certain taboo thoughts or experiences for the audience. By making them public it releases the audience in a certain way. You get your best laughs when you shock the audience with something they've been thinking but have never been able to verbalize or express. Or didn't even know they were thinking, maybe. It's somehow consistent with a secret thought or an embarrassment that they understand. To simply insult them or abuse them without context or relevance or resonance doesn't really work.

—Harold Ramis

and created my fate by making an initial choice that leads me through a specific world with specific people. And if, by the end, I still hated my scene, thankfully I'll never see it again. Unless someone taped it for posterity and I'm fucked. I'm in hell. Ain't it grand?

—Susan Messing

Forming Opinions

"What do you want to say?" "What makes you angry?" "What do you care about?" These are the questions that are posed to each Second City ensemble at the beginning of every new rehearsal process. There is a mandate on our stages that the work be not just funny but also satirical. It's a tremendous privilege to get up onstage every night and share your thoughts and feelings on events in the world with an audience. I remember Stephen Colbert expressing great frustration when a major political scandal broke shortly after he had left the Chicago Mainstage cast—"I have something I want to say about it and I want to do it onstage."

In order to help carry forth the tradition of topical, social, and political commentary as represented by the original Second City milieu, everybody should *read* daily newspapers, weekly magazines, business and science journals, right- and left-wing publications, commentary, and *Doonesbury. Watch* TV. Not only the shows that you prefer but also the programs that are most highly rated in the Nielsens.

Find a way to *personalize* at least one side of any aspect of what you are being exposed to and *discuss, argue,* and *share* with fellow players, friends, and acquaintances whatever insights you are getting; whatever "slant," ironic or angry, should be/could be material for the improv set.

Continuing offstage engagement will help you *confront* and *refine* your newly forming (or firming) opinions, develop the ongoing mindset, and let you relax enough so that you can "pop" within the context of scene forming, emotional content, character, ideation, music styles, and so on. By "pop" I mean have that moment in performance whereby your personality communicates with the audience in a quantum-leap, multilevel expression that is at once highly personal and yet clearly objective, sophisticated, and undeniably uninhibited.

After personalizing all this input (pop culture, best sellers, TV, news, and music) you can apply it consciously to a scene or scenario, building blackouts or launching into any of the "spot" improvs. You will gain relaxation and trust, knowing that the time put in on these attitudes, opinions, and insights will come forth intuitively. In other words, *stoke the furnace that is your mind (personality)* and the form this energy takes will surprise and please you because it will be coming from a committed frame of reference. I believe that all great improvisers should be committed. Pun intended!

Finally, don't lay a trip on yourself by being too judgmental while trying out these new wings. Agree with your emerging expression! Who knows where it will take you? You will be able to count on it with more ease as you keep using it. If you are unhappy with what comes at first, remember the greatest four-letter word in show business . . . *next!*

—*Avery Schreiber*

Finding Scenic Point of View

Once you know what you want to say, the next bit, which is nearly as difficult, is finding a way to say it scenically. After all, we don't just get up onstage and harangue the audience with our opinions; we put those opinions in context and improvise their consequences. Sandra Balcovske has enormous experience assisting performers in this difficult task. She has directed numerous productions on the Toronto Mainstage and served as artistic director for our theater there as well.

What is scenic point of view? Where do we find it?

For my purposes, scenic point of view is the raison d'être of the scene. It is why the scene exists. It is the overriding notion that the audience is meant to take from the scene. Scenic point of view can be anything from a harsh indictment of a political action to a gentle observation about human nature.

In the process of putting up a show from improvised material, the scenic point of view is often decided beforehand and/or developed through repeated improvisations. A rough gem is evident either in the premise of the scene or in the initial improvisation and honed into a show-worthy

There's a common perception abroad that we are a political theater. That was never true. Certainly, at election times and times like you mentioned, we have more political content but politics is only part of life. Working is part of life. Marriage is part of life. Dating is part of life. All of these things are subjects at Second City, and as long as you have an ironic approach and you're reflecting what's going on in the world and in your generation, it's political.

—*Bernie Sahlins*

piece. But in the actual process of improvising—whether to develop material or as an end in itself—the scenic point of view must be created onstage. So how do we increase our odds of doing that successfully?

For those of us lucky enough to have created or observed one of those improvisations that has rhythm and flow, entertaining content, and a satisfying conclusion, it can seem like magic. But a good magician spends hours practicing sleight of hand. What can the improviser do? What is scenic point of view made of? Is it possible to practice the constituent parts of creating scenic "magic"?

For me, the scenic point of view arises from the actions and point of view of the characters in the scene. The point of view of the scene need not be held by all or indeed any of the characters, particularly for the creation of satire, irony, and whatever we're calling "conflict" these days. A scene about hatred doesn't have to have a single hateful thing said or done. The basic building block of scenic point of view is character—a very particular person who can be put in any particular time and place.

So what can the improviser practice? He can practice creating very particular people. People with passions, beliefs, problems, ideas, achievements, and a psychology—people who are in a mood or emotional state, people with an inner life. The improviser can practice naming and owning these characters. The improviser can practice making strong choices about these people, their actions, and their behaviors, and recognize that strong choices do not necessarily equal huge choices. The improviser can practice being a person who keenly observes detail, a person who is curious about the world, a person with a wide and varied reference level, a person with a desire to communicate. In short, the improviser can practice having a personal point of view on any subject, a skill that can be honed at the dinner table any night of the week.

When working with a group over a period of time (be that a fifty-five-minute long-form Harold or a year at Second City), the improviser can repeat characters. This gives her fellow players a chance to work with the character in different situations and get to know the person being created. The character becomes a known quantity, and the whole group can participate in the scenic use of the character—including the character in the initial premise or calling the character into a scene. This can be a shortcut to finding a scenic point of view. Why? Because when an actor sees that

"Mindy the overachiever" or "Joe the closet redneck" is in the scene, that actor has a frame of reference. Whether the scene is about Mindy working the line at GM or Joe running a day-care center, that character is not a complete stranger. There are known buttons to be pushed. It is in the pushing of these buttons (known, assumed, offered, or discovered) that the scene, and therefore the scenic point of view, arises.

How do we develop scenic point of view? We really see and listen to the characters present onstage. We choose and use our own character to feed the situation and the relationship(s). In heightening and exploring the premise or the offer on the table, we make sure the emotional and physical action of the scene progresses. Our dialogue supports the action either directly or indirectly, and scenic point of view arises from these elements. When Mindy and Joe go to a sushi restaurant on the suggestion of "first date," the scenic point of view could end up being anything from the need for gun control to the joys of stunt eating. The scene itself can be a love scene, a teaching scene, or a rock opera with a dream sequence. It's what arises out of the action and dialogue that creates scenic point of view.

When working from audience suggestions, character choices are key to finding scenic point of view. What particular choices will feed an interaction with, relationship with, or opinion about the suggested issue/occupation/object? How does this character best participate in this situation and location to create a scene that entertains, elucidates, or provokes? Fortunately and unfortunately, the answer to this last question is all in the specifics of the moment, and examples will never amount to a rule. It might have been better for Mindy to order the blowfish or Joe to have a Vietnam flashback, but in improvisation as in life, we don't know the road not taken. Except of course if we have another set tomorrow night.

Have fun, mean well, and remember that for every rule there is a counterexample.

—*Sandra Balcovske*

Finding Your Voice

For years, a running joke in the improv community was that the classic cast of improvisers was "white guys in neckties," and even now if you look around a typical improv classroom you see a lot of white male faces (although there are fewer ties and a lot more backward baseball caps). In the past, when women and minorities were members of improv ensembles they often seemed relegated to playing secondary roles or improvising in a world defined by the straight white males in the ensemble.

Slowly but surely, the situation is changing for the better. Gayco Productions, which began as a Second City Training Center workshop, recently celebrated its fifth anniversary. At our Training Center theater, Donny's Skybox, we have had shows dedicated to black performers, Hispanic performers, and all-female groups. All of the Chicago-based touring companies now contain equal numbers of men and women. And due to executive producer Andrew Alexander's passion for outreach and inclusion there are now more minority performers on resident stages at Second City than ever before.

But presence is only part of the issue. Once the performers are in place, the real work begins—making that presence meaningful in the material created on our stages. Keegan-Michael Key has been working on Second City stages for more than five years now, first at our location in Detroit and more recently at The Second City ETC in Chicago, where he was nominated for a Jeff Award for his work in the revue Holy War, Batman!, *in which he played a black Jesus, a normal guy stuck at a folk concert, and a Pakistani cab driver dealing with the aftereffects of September 11.*

How do you find your voice as a person of color in improvisational theater? As I began to contemplate this inquiry it was met with anxiety. Why are they asking me this question!? I am a thirty-one-year-old male. I'm half black and half white. I was primarily raised by a white woman who grew up on a farm in northern Illinois. I spent my formative years in a mostly white, definitely suburban high school. I have often felt guilty about not spending more time with African American people. I don't listen to Erykah Badu or Ja Rule every day. I don't play dominoes. I don't wear baggy jeans. I married a white woman! In fact, I have felt guilty about not experiencing more racism in my life. As I began to reflect more on the answer, something a colleague of mine once said popped into my head: "If you're black and in a scene then the scene is about race."

I agree with this statement. Whether conscious or otherwise, your ethnicity will resonate with an audience. Due to the sociological underpinnings of our culture it is unavoidable for an American to ignore the dynamic of a black person and a white person onstage together. My guilt about not being "more black" *is* part of my black experience. With that said, my initial response to the above question is find your voice by being yourself, no matter what your melanin count is. No one person's experience is "blacker" or more Hispanic than the next. You are not more Chinese than your neighbor. Life experiences are intrinsically filtered through how you appear, just as much as how you were raised or taught.

Therefore, how you improvise should not be compromised. Improvisation as a culture strives to find some absolutes within itself. We all agree that there is some form of agreement, that we are creating and establishing something together. No matter what nomenclature you use, the basic concepts are the same. So bring your voice to your skill.

Let's talk about what your "voice" is for a moment. In my opinion, our voice is our personal outlook and point of view on the world, manifested through performance. We take our opinions and dramatize them, so as to provoke thought, emotion, and perhaps change in others. The "how" of our improvisation should remain the same. It is not the art that changes but the artist. Voice also pertains to the type of scenes you enjoy playing: do you take more pleasure in physical comedy or wordplay? You may be very adept at silent scenes. Your scenic preferences become part of your signature. To get back to our question, I believe that it is what comes before our craft that is unique.

When you are trying to find your voice, I caution you not to hold on to notions of what you may think you are supposed to do. "I'm Hispanic, but I don't speak Spanish, so why should I perform scenes about my ethnicity?" Your experience is your experience. How do you struggle with not speaking Spanish? Use the improvisational tools you've learned to dramatize that. Sometimes, we feel we must show a blind deference to our elders or try to duplicate their experiences. I say put forth your reactions to your elders and their lives. Do you admire them or disapprove of them? One of the best ways for us to seek our voice is to observe your reactions to what other people do, and if you are aware enough, others' reactions to what you do. How we feel about a given word or action informs us as to what our opinions of life are.

When I have been in the process of writing a show, I often meditate on certain questions to get my mind working in a particular way. These questions typically deal with my natural impulses toward what I witness and observe in this life. What do I think people's expectations of me are? What makes me angry about being a person of color? What about stereotypes do I believe are true? Are there generalizations about my race that I think are true? As you ask one question of yourself more will start toppling out of you.

I think it's important to mention that when you are improvising you should not force these questions or answers to the forefront of your mind. If you find yourself in a position where your race may enhance the scene then react accordingly. You will find that you react from your own truth. There is no right way to do it. There is no quota of how many angry young black men you have to play in a week's worth of sets; if that is what comes to you, then pursue it. If there is a person in your life who has made you look at your life in a different way in regard to race, I invite you to create a character based on how you feel about the qualities he or she possesses. It is not an impersonation we're after, but a representation of someone's essence. You create the character by examining what it was about the person that seized your imagination, and using that as the thrust of the character's life onstage.

—*Keegan-Michael Key*

AN IMPROVISATIONAL ALMANAC: PART THREE

Invest a great deal of importance in what you are doing, saying, choosing, and reacting to.

✦ ✦ ✦

Become a part of the whole. Help out in any way that you can. Be each other's stage managers. Help and be helped. It's okay to not be Superman all the time.

✦ ✦ ✦

Once you are playing onstage, take on a competence at something, with the confidence of an expert, at whatever you are doing.

✦ ✦ ✦

To help find an end to the scene, look to the beginning.

✦ ✦ ✦

As soon as a player starts to tell jokes, he starts to treat the other actors as objects. Comments on the scene or to the audience are not part of the scene and can be very detrimental to the scene reality. They are also subtle displays of not trusting. This is also a sign of the player going into his head to solve the problem, rather than trusting the focus and the other players. The stronger improvisers try to make use of the discoveries in the environment, using objects or details.

✦ ✦ ✦

Try not to tell; try to show.

✦ ✦ ✦

Do not talk about what you are doing.

✦ ✦ ✦

For heightened object work, focus on the object. Give it time, weight, space, shape, and detail. This will help the object take on more reality and the audience will appreciate your talent more.

❧ ❧ ❧

We create the rules that the audience feels uncomfortable for us in.

❧ ❧ ❧

There is a great deal of difference between improvising and making things up. "Let's pretend" as we played it when we were younger is only the doorway to creating the realities of the stage. One can feel the vast difference between inventing or thinking and the incredible state of improvisation.

❧ ❧ ❧

It's interesting how "dull" can be interesting.

❧ ❧ ❧

Improvising is a bit like Zen archery. One must misdirect oneself to be on target.

❧ ❧ ❧

Satire and Humor = Tragedy + Time. It is strange how we accomplish this. Humans are unique in their ability to laugh at things, and after a very sad or tragic event, with some interval of time, we can find some humor in it to help ease the burden of grief.

❧ ❧ ❧

We can handle conflict or disagreement if it is all contained within a larger overall agreement between the players. Do not argue just to argue, and find the solution if you must disagree.

❧ ❧ ❧

Do not attempt to emotionally affect the audience, unless the work being done at that time demands it. This is not to say that we do not want to affect the audience, but we do not want to hit them over the head with the message. Again, assume their intelligence will allow them to feel for themselves.

❧ ❧ ❧

There are no holds barred; anything can happen and should—it's just a matter of when the holds are used.

❧ ❧ ❧

Occasionally play against your feelings. Surprise yourself and the audience at the same time. This will help keep the audience from getting ahead of you.

⊸ ⊸ ⊸

Remember to give and take with equal intensity.

⊸ ⊸ ⊸

Share the responsibilities for the success of the scene. To use the analogy of a motor driving a car, if there are six people onstage, then each person is like a piston and responsible for one-sixth of the scene. You may be the scene leader or motor, but you can't do it all by yourself.

⊸ ⊸ ⊸

Incorporate the moments of discovery from the past into the institution of the future; that is, learn from the mistakes of the past to help improve your future.

⊸ ⊸ ⊸

What we are is infinitely more interesting than who we are.

⊸ ⊸ ⊸

Try to end just before you peak.

⊸ ⊸ ⊸

Ideas reveal more when they are acted upon than when they are discussed. The rule of threes is inflexible. If something is done twice, it must be done a third time.

⊸ ⊸ ⊸

If you are bored, your audience is also bored and this may mean you are not building anything. You can do just about anything to an audience— scare them, disgust them, please them, amuse them—but try to never ever bore them.

CHAPTER FOUR: **IMPROVISATION AND ACTING**

Until I got here, the written word in a play (new or old) was sacrosanct. It came down from God. Well, it went two ways. First of all, I felt like I could start to look at a script and say, "Wait a minute, this doesn't make any sense. I don't care if he is a hot writer, it doesn't make any sense." Conversely, I remember looking at written transcripts of scenes we did at Second City that were considered minor masterpieces. When they were written down on paper, they looked like hash! It looked like nonsense! I realize the incredible investment of persona or acting technique that went into a lot of the scenes when nothing was there. It gave me a sense of how much more important an actor was in terms of his or her nuances than what was necessarily in print or a script. It went both ways.

—*Alan Arkin*

Perhaps one of the most interesting things about improvisation is the discovery of how useful its theory and practice are in so many different areas and disciplines. Improvisation can exist on its own as an art form in performance. And of course you can use improvisation to create sketch comedy as Second City has done on its resident stages for nearly forty-five years. There are applications to life and business practice—it is not unusual for a student in the beginning program at the Training Center to relate a story of feeling stuck at work, lacking respect from colleagues or supervisors, unable to get a promotion, and then after six months or so in classes, suddenly it all seemed to turn around. Work became easier and more fluid, interactions with bosses and peers took on a new tone, and the student finds herself on a track to "move up." Our corporate division, Second City Communications, is well aware of these applications to job performance and has had great success providing improvisational training to corporations and businesses all over the country.

In the midst of all this, it is easy to neglect the original intention behind Viola Spolin's improvisational theory—training actors to work with text. Martin de Maat used to suggest that improvisation would be the "twenty-first-century school of acting." And there are indications that this is increasingly true. Not only have actors trained in improvisation gone on to success in theater, television, and film but many colleges and universities are beginning to recognize that work in improvisation is more than just "fun and games"—it is intensely valuable in its applications to text work. In New York, Viola's son and Second City cofounder Paul Sills lectures and leads training in improvisation at the New Actors Workshop, a school he helped found with Mike Nichols and George Morrison. In Chicago, Columbia College, one of the largest theater programs in the country, bases much of its acting training in improvisation.

Building a Character within an Ensemble through the Games

Sheldon Patinkin is the chairman of the Columbia College theater department. He has been a part of Second City from the very beginning. He served as artistic director from 1960 until 1968, directed and taught at our location in Toronto, and was one of the original writers and producers for SCTV. He developed the Training Center in Chicago and currently serves as artistic consultant for The Second City theaters.

I have been lucky enough to be able to work closely with Sheldon at Second City and under his direction at Columbia College. Sheldon is not only one of the smartest people I know; he understands the art of directing sketch comedy revue as well as anyone alive today. He often comes to see the resident company shows shortly before opening to give notes to the director. Sheldon is the master of the simple note that makes all the difference in the scene.

During the first show I directed for Second City, I was struggling with a musical closer; the cast loved performing the number but it just wasn't funny. Sheldon's note was brief—"Change 'is' to 'was' in the last verse"; I made the change and immediately the song got the laughs it never got before.

Sheldon influenced the evolution of another Chicago theater institution —the famed Steppenwolf Theatre Ensemble, whose members include John Malkovich, Jeff Perry, Laurie Metcalf, and Gary Sinise. While they were still based in Highland Park, he came out and taught the group workshops in improvisation—workshops that Steppenwolf members claim had a transformative effect on their work individually and as an ensemble.

I've had Hollywood directors tell me that you can always tell a Second City actor; he looks at the other guy's parts as well as his own. And what's important about being in an ensemble is not the feeling of fellowship or the warm feeling around the cockles of the heart, but the fact that the way your fellow actor acts in relation to you determines your character.

—*Bernie Sahlins*

In the midsixties, while I was the director of Second City and, along with Jo Forsberg, one of the improv teachers training people in the skills involved in being funny on your feet without swearing or dropping your pants—long before there was an official Second City Training Center or even a Players Workshop—Paul Sills decided he wanted to see what happened when you applied the rules of many of his mother Viola Spolin's improvisational games on an already existing text. Since a group of people playing the games together invariably creates an ensemble, why not see what happens when playing them on the text of an ensemble-driven play? We recruited a cast for Chekhov's *The Cherry Orchard*. Paul felt there should be no directors, only players, so we were both part of the cast against my better judgment and talent; but since we weren't going to perform it for an audience, okay. Paul played the guy who ends up buying the orchard, and I played the perpetual student.

For three nights a week for most of a year, we played many of Viola's games on every scene in the play. It all came together for me one night playing the game Contact on the third-act scene between the student and Madame Ranevskaya. The rule of Contact is that you can't talk unless you've first made *justified* physical contact with the person you're talking to. There's a stage direction at the top of one of the student's speeches that says he delivers it "in tears." In all the times we'd worked on the scene, I couldn't find any reason to be in tears and didn't want to fake it, so I never cried. Then we played it in Contact and I burst into tears on making contact before saying the line. (I won't say what reason I found, since it's probably not what Chekhov had in mind.)

The point is that in Contact, you know how it feels to need to touch the other character, how it feels to actually touch the other character, and how the other character feels being touched by you. I soon realized that the games could supply something otherwise lacking in the training of actors, most particularly by focusing concern on what's going on between the characters, whether verbalized or not. When I later started teaching acting classes, a lot of my techniques came from that *Cherry Orchard* experiment, and I therefore have the students play games before starting work on scripted scenes. (The exercises and games I use are based on Viola's, but they're often in less than their purest form.) And when I teach improv classes now, they're not for people who want to learn how to improvise; they're for people who want to learn more about acting. In fact, I immediately assure them that I'm not looking for good scenes (scenes that might be repeatable and end up in a show), and that they're not obligated to be funny.

Somewhere around the middle of the first acting class, it's usually time for the Bernhardt-Duse-Stanislavsky lecture. Briefly (and simplistically), Stanislavsky, both as actor and director, was unhappy with the usual kind of acting of his day, with the famed French actress Sarah Bernhardt as the best example. She played emotions, and, boy, did she play them. She also was always stage center, never turned her back to the audience when speaking, rarely looked at the other actors, continued acting after she lost a leg, even played Hamlet with the wooden leg, and, for good measure, slept in a silk-lined coffin—a true nineteenth-century star. (It's now called "indicating," or "playing results." It's also called hammy, selfish, and a lot worse.) But then there was the famed Italian actress Eleanora Duse, who fascinated Stanislavsky. Her performances were far more naturalistic, more believable; furthermore, she was able to blush when it was appropriate for her character to blush. (She apparently found it appropriate at least once in every role she played.) Now Stanislavsky knew that you can't *act* a blush. To make a long story too short, he understood that in order to be able to blush, you have to play the circumstances that produce the blush, and to get there you have to play the circumstances that produce an emotion, not the emotion itself. Thus the foundations of almost all contemporary acting styles and training are based on Stanislavsky, no matter how distantly.

Most acting systems are about teaching the actor how to think and feel in character in order to become the character (rather than turning the character into the actor, as was the case with many early Method actors, but I won't go into my rant about that). However, what they don't usually concentrate on enough is what's going on *between* the characters, and how much of your focus has to be on the others. Since I usually teach people who've already had training, I concentrate less on the character's "spine" (your given circumstances and general wants from life) and far more on how that spine produces what your character wants from the other characters from moment to moment when you're onstage with them, and why you want these things. (It's the "why" that usually connects back to the character's spine.) Playing Viola's games helps you learn how to play moment to moment. After all, in an improv you don't know what the next moment is unless you're listening to, watching, and reacting to the others. And the games help you learn how to break more of your focus off yourself, how to give as well as take, how to receive as well as give, and how to know not just what you need from the others, but also what the others need from you, whether your character is willing to give it or not. In other words, the games help an actor understand how to be part of an ensemble, where everyone is alive to everyone else every moment they're onstage together.

For me, an ideal class has twelve students, which means you can do teams of two, three, four, and six, depending on the exercise or game. I start the first class by having all the students do a Space Walk, moving through the acting space, getting them to feel their whole body moving through the space—not visualizing it, not conceptualizing it, feeling it. After a while, they start moving through the space in slow motion, then slower, then slower still, all the time *feeling* their bodies pushing through the space. Then it's back to normal speed, this time making eye contact with all the others moving through the space with them, making sure that they both see and be seen, and eventually see and be seen head to toe. They continue seeing and being seen as they move faster, then faster, then faster still. Then they freeze while I explain Stage Picture: "With one movement up, down, sideways, or whatever, when I call 'Stage Picture,' I want to be able to see everyone's face from where I'm standing." If they don't accomplish it, they have to start moving around again at top speed, freeze, "Stage Picture," until they get it right. Of course, I try to stand where it will be most difficult for them to get it right. So now they've gotten themselves into the space and have started to build an awareness of the others.

I do a Space Walk at the beginning of every class, with variations. In the second class, after Stage Picture, they start moving around at normal speed again for a little while, seeing and being seen head to toe; then they freeze, close their eyes, relax, keep their eyes closed, and change something about their appearance—what they're wearing, their hair, or whatever. (Not their posture.) After everyone has made some change, they open their eyes and move around, seeing if they can figure out what each person has changed, without saying it. Then we go around the group, calling out each person's change. In the third class, instead of moving faster after slow motion, they continue moving normally, seeing and being seen; then they close their eyes and continue moving normally. When they come in contact with someone, they have to stop and, with eyes still closed, figure out who it is. When they know, they continue moving till the next contact, and so on. *No sounds.* After enough of this, they go back to moving around with their eyes still closed but ignore when they come in contact and just keep moving. Then they freeze, eyes still closed, and see if they know where they are in the room, if someone is near them, and if so, who. When they think they know, or have given up, they can open their eyes but have to remain still till everyone's eyes are open. Usually there's one person left with his or her eyes still closed, and I signal the others to quietly surround him or her so that when he or she opens his or her eyes, everyone's looking at him or her. (I'll stop being politically correct now and just sort of alternate pronouns.) In other classes they do Space Walk changing their centers of gravity and initiating movement with some other part of their bodies, or move through the space as a character they're working on, whatever. Always it includes seeing and being seen head to toe by the rest of by what is now an ensemble.

After Space Walk, they count off into two groups of six, and each team plays Give and Take while the other team serves as a *quiet* audience. It's an exercise with a simple rule and is, for me, the skeleton of everything there is to know about being part of an ensemble. The rule is that only one person can be in motion at a time. All six begin in a frozen position, then one of them is told to start motion while the others remain frozen—all they can move are their eyes. Motion moves to another player in one of two ways: either the person in motion gives it by freezing in front of someone who must immediately start moving, though not necessarily by continuing the giver's motion, or someone who's frozen begins to move and the person in motion has to freeze instantly. No one is to make sounds. I side-coach when someone's arms keep moving after she's frozen, when someone continues for a step or two after the motion has been taken from him, when there's too much give and not enough take or vice versa, and so on. I'll also occasionally ask the person in motion to give it to the person who's been frozen the longest. Each team continues playing for several minutes—at least until they all get it right. They do this exercise each class after Space Walk for two or three classes in a row, and periodically throughout the rest of the classes. By the third class, after the second team has been playing it long enough, I add the first team one at a time by telling each of them to join by taking the motion. Soon the whole class/ensemble is playing it together.

Unlike Viola and Paul, I find it helpful to talk a bit about the purposes and results of some of the games and exercises. After the first time they play Give and Take, we talk for a while about what they found most difficult to accomplish while playing: knowing when it's been taken from you? freezing completely? taking immediately when it's been given to you? taking? giving? Things to know about yourself. We also talk about the exercise as the skeleton of being part of an ensemble: two people moving at the same time is a dialogue overlap (which can be intentional in a play but never in Give and Take); not knowing who's been frozen the longest; not knowing when someone else has taken focus; not making sure the person in focus knows that you're taking focus; and so on. In other words, Give and Take is the beginning of learning to split your focus so that you know what's going on all around you—essential to being part of an ensemble.

Next is Bus Stop, a basic exercise in building a character. Again the students count off into two teams of six. About midway upstage, we set up six chairs (with backs and without arms) in a straight line, nearly touching each other and facing the audience. The first team sits on the chairs; the other team is the audience. The first team is told to silently pick an age (above puberty and below senility, please) and an occupation they wish to become. I side-coach them into silently physicalizing the age, moving from toes to head, including the face and the five senses. Then they add the physicalization of the occupation through these questions: "What parts of your body work better because this is your occupation? What parts are in

There are applications to everything from Second City stuff. Writing, obviously. It's interesting how Paul [Sills] brought it to use in a regular play. You can't change the lines every night, but you can bring that sense of spontaneity. He once said, "There's no laughter like the explosion of laughter after improvisation." To those people paying their money there, it's not important that you have done this two hundred times before. It's important that they're seeing it for their first and only time and you make it seem like it's the first and only time. I think there are applications here that bring freshness to the interpretation of the same lines. So what if the prop isn't exactly in the same place? What if you change a little bit of the way you're doing it? It makes it more interesting. It applies to almost everything.

—*Robert Klein*

less good tune? What does this occupation do to your view of the world and of the people in it?" Then they're told they're at a bus stop, where the bus will be coming from, where it will stop, and that it's morning. Then they answer the following questions silently: "Where are you coming from? How do you feel about where you're coming from? Where are you going to? How do you feel about where you're going to? How do you feel about having to take a bus?"—that is, basic given circumstances. They make eye contact with the others at the bus stop, see and be seen, but without forming relationships, and no talking. Then "The bus is a block away." After a while "The bus is half a block away." After a while, "The bus is arriving. Get up and catch the bus." Once they're all up and waiting, probably in line, either the bus goes by without stopping or the bus is stalled in traffic. After another while, another bus or the original bus is arriving. Then "The bus is here, get on the bus one at a time, go back to your original seat, hold on to your character, and listen to what's about to be said without reacting." The audience is asked to say what they got as the age and occupation of each of the players. (It's important to realize that it can usually only be done in age categories and in types of occupations such as blue collar, white collar, midrange executive, and so on, though sometimes the audience can get much more exact than that.) The players take what they've heard and make adjustments if the audience didn't get it right, including mimed props if they'll help. Then they go back to waiting for the bus, getting on the bus, going back to the seats, and once again hearing what the audience thinks each player's age and occupation is, followed by the player saying what it is. Usually whatever adjustments the players make, if any are needed, are more specific, though also often more clichéd in order to make things clearer without dialogue or context.

This exercise is a minimal start at building the physical life of a character, since how you feel about yourself affects how you look, how you look affects how you feel about yourself, and both affect what you want from life and what you want from others. Again, most acting classes deal far more with the inner than with the outer life, yet both are nearly equally important to building a character rather than making the character into yourself. The physical life of your character includes body language: how and when to gesture, how to sit, what kind of stride to take when walking, general posture, what kind of clothing your character is wearing and how that affects movement and posture, and so on. It also includes what kind of voice and vocal range to use. Since much of this is found through trial and error, it's best to start on it at more or less the same time you're building the inside. Sometimes it helps to go to the zoo, find an animal or bird that somehow reminds you of the character, and watch it. Then—back home, please—be the animal (including the face), move around like it, and gradually humanize it until you're moving like a person but retaining whatever makes sense of the physical characteristics of the animal.

I think it's valuable to find at least one minor physical difference between the actor and the character; it makes getting into character easier. I don't mean a limp or a lisp; it's rarely necessary to go to an extreme. But something, no matter how slight, that makes you feel you're in your character's body and voice. Work in front of a full-length mirror; record yourself. (Remember, if you don't like what you see or hear, it's not the fault of the mirror or the tape recorder.) Better still, have someone videotape you so you can watch yourself after you've done it rather than while you're doing it. Spending time in front of a mirror or a camera, seeing how you look this way and that way, is no longer vanity; it's work. If your facial expressions look forced, it's because you haven't spent enough time in front of your mirror till you know by muscle control alone how big to make the face so that it looks real rather than mugged. Everything to do with examining how you look, how you could look, how you speak, how you could speak, how you move, how you could move, how you gesture, how you could gesture is work and has to be reapplied to every new character.

So much for opening warm-ups, exercises, and talks. It's time for the first game, which means planning a scene. There are several categories to be decided on while a team is planning, some depending on the game, some for any game. Most of the language is from Viola, created originally for teaching children, and therefore very simple.

The Who is who you are—your character, including such obvious givens as age, education, occupation, sexual orientation, marital status, and so on.

The Where is where the scene takes place, including entrances, furniture, windows, appliances, or machinery, everything permanently there. (It's best to draw it out so everyone on the team has it clearly in mind, since they can only use chairs and maybe a table, though for Viola and Paul it's only chairs. Sometimes I think it would be best not to mime props, most actors are so bad at it.)

The What is a mutual physical activity everyone can participate in during the scene, though it's not necessary always to be doing it, or that everyone be doing it at the same time. Discussing something isn't a physical activity. Fishing isn't mutual unless there's only one pole or it's a fishing class. Sports, cards, and board games are hard to mime. You get the idea.

The opening emotional state, including why your character is in it, is exactly that. Be in it before starting the scene, and be able to heighten it, lessen it, or change it soon after the scene begins. (I assume actors know what to use to get themselves into an opening emotional state. I also assume they know not to tell anyone what they use, or it'll stop working for them. No one knows why.)

The want is what your character wants from each of the other characters, and the why is why he wants it. (Like so much acting language, the concept has many other words for the same thing depending on the acting system being taught, including *objective, intention, motivation,* and so on.) There are two kinds of wants. Outer wants are ones you can directly ask for; in a script, they're probably in the dialogue, although you can ask for a light for a cigarette without saying anything, you can offer someone a chair or food or a poisoned drink without saying anything, and so on. Inner wants are harder or impossible to ask for in the circumstances, so that you have to try to get them without directly asking for them—things like love, sex, money, divorce, admission of guilt, and so on. In a script they're subtext and, if finally verbalized, only under great duress. For a script, choose and play wants, both outer and inner, that help you understand why this is the next moment. And don't be satisfied with what already works; keep on looking for more layers, more possible moment-to-moment choices. The worst that can happen is that something you try doesn't work; so you won't try that one again. Big deal. Unless you're willing to be wrong, you won't try things that might be right for a particular moment. Better to be an asshole than a chickenshit.

Figuring out more wants to try is mostly an actor's homework rather than something you get directed into during rehearsals—just like learning lines. (It's important to learn lines early, by rote, in a monotone, and to be able to say them faster than you'll ever deliver them, so that you're not memorizing line readings, just the words themselves, since the line readings must come as responses to the others' line readings and physical behavior.) Until the lines are memorized, you can't genuinely start listening to and seeing the others, and therefore can't really know how what you're playing is being received. The fluctuating circumstances of each moment onstage produce your character's fluctuating emotional states, and the fluctuating emotional states are caused by how near or far your character is from getting what she wants from the other characters onstage at each moment, then gauging how to proceed accordingly. In other words, you must not only know what your character wants from life and from each of the other characters, you must also be fully present to each moment in order to know how it affects those wants. That's the most exciting part of the work. You should also have at least one inner want going for each other character onstage with you, even if you ultimately have to ask for it. Then you're playing subtext, which always makes your character more interesting by giving him more depth and dimension; something more is going on inside than he's saying. (By the fourth improv class, a lot of our focus is on planning and playing inner wants.)

Many directors go into the first day of rehearsal knowing what the spine of the play is for them—what the play is about for them, what it's saying to them. This is usually communicated to the actors. (If it's not, I don't think you should ask; the director may not work that way, may not have thought about the play that way, and you might piss her off. Not a good way to start.) The director may also know what the spine of each character is and how it fits into the spine of the play. How much of this he chooses to communicate to the actors is a variable. As an actor, you don't have to know what the director sees as the theme of the play and how your character fits into said theme, but as part of an ensemble, it helps. It helps you understand where focus is from moment to moment and how your character contributes to it.

I don't think actors are dumb. I think they have to be smart, especially to be really good, though I've worked with exceptions. The more you know about the whole thing, the more you understand what your job is in it from moment to moment. And the more you understand what your job is in it, the more you can play each moment, whether you're the focus of that moment or not.

There's another thing that's unique to Second City and improvisational actors. I've done a lot of directing over the years and whenever somebody from Second City would come in and read a part, they would know exactly what their function was in the entirety of the play (unlike almost any other actors I've ever worked with). Most of the actors I know who haven't worked in this way come in and they're myopic. They know what they want to do and it may have nothing to do with what anybody else is doing in the play. Second City actors will immediately save a week's time because they know what their function is in the play. They have their antenna up for what the other actors are doing and need. Almost invariably.

—Alan Arkin

If there's time for planning and playing two games in the first class, I start with Who Am I? Count off into groups of three. Each team chooses one of the three to leave the room while the other two plan the following information for all three: who the third person is and who they are in relationship to her and to each other, where they are, and something all three are waiting for that will not happen during the scene. The Whos are to be relationships—friends, relatives, coworkers, and so on. What they're all waiting for can't be something like an agent and a manager with a rock star, waiting for her to sign a contract, because the rock star isn't waiting for that. Here are a couple of examples I'd rather never see again: triplets waiting to be born, siblings waiting for Santa Claus, parents and child waiting to see the principal. The scene must then be played as if all three of the players know all the planned information. If the person who doesn't know says something that doesn't fit the circumstances, the others must correct her in character *in dialogue,* or she'll think what she said is correct. The scene is over when she says, *in dialogue,* who she is, who the other two are in relationship to her, where they are, and what they're all waiting for. No one is to ask questions—the two who know because she doesn't know, the one who doesn't know because she's supposed to know. It's all about listening, responding, and helping. Of course, if you help too much too soon, it'll be a very short scene.

If there's time for planning and playing only one game, I save Who Am I? for the second class and proceed directly to Word Game. Word Game is a sort of charades game, and a good way to introduce a class to how to plan a scene, since the subject matter is a given. Count off into two teams of six. Each team is to pick a word that can itself be divided into two words, though not a compound word like *baseball* or *lunchtime.* They should rather choose words like *masterful, pristine, expectorate, Sheldon,* or—with a little stretching—words like *syllable* ("silly-bull") or *fanny* ("fan-knee"). Don't spend a lot of time picking the word; it's not important. Then divide the word into its two halves, and for each half, pick Whos, Whats, and Wheres that will illustrate it *without actually saying it.* After the teams have finished planning, each team does both words in order, and the audience has to guess the word *after* both scenes have been performed.

The first time the class plays Word Game, the scenes are usually pretty short, pretty silly, and not very good. Not a problem. I point out to them that I purposely left out planning wants, and that therefore they had nothing much to do onstage but illustrate the word. In the second class, they play Word Game again, but this time they're also told to plan an outer want for each of the other characters in the scene and know why they want it, and they're to tell each other their wants as part of the planning. It can be the same want for all (though that's not really a good idea), the same want for some, or different wants for each. The scenes get longer and better. After the audience guesses the word, they're asked if they could tell what wants were being played.

Next time they play Word Game, one of their words has to be played in gibberish. First they do Gibberish Sell: each of them invents a one-minute commercial for a product they have to sell to the class in gibberish. It's also a good idea to do Gibberish Story: each of them tells a partner in gibberish about some incident in his life, preferably fairly brief; when the story is finished, the partner tells the story to the audience in English.

After three or at most four times of playing Word Game, they're ready to plan scenes without the crutch of tying them to a word. They're also ready to start playing inner wants, which they are told to invent for each of the other players as part of the planning, but unlike the Who, What, Where, and outer wants, they're *not* to tell each other their inner wants. (By then, they should also be preparing opening emotional states and why they're in them.) With inner wants, it's usually better to start with no more than three or four on a team. (I rarely ask students to plan two-person scenes, which aren't as much help in building ensemble techniques.) One of the most helpful inner-wants games is when the rule of the game requires each player to figure out and say in dialogue what the other players' inner wants are for her.

Inventing wants for an improv is difficult at first. The more important to you your wants are—the higher the stakes—the more likely you are to find the most dramatic and interesting ways of pursuing them, relaxing, pressurizing, or changing your tactics as you realize how close or far you are from getting them. It's also important to phrase wants as positives, particularly in improvs. Instead of "I want you out of my life," which means you want the actor to leave the stage, what could he do that would make it all right for him to stay in your character's life? You're not likely to get it, but that's what you've got to work for, for as long as possible. Wants should never be phrased with *not*s and *don't*s. Find the positive and don't give up on it until there's no hope left. And if you get a want, invent another one to play on the spot, or you'll lose focus on that person.

Along with Contact, here are some of the other exercises and games we play for building ensemble techniques during the time we have:

What's Beyond? Each student, one at a time, enters from one side of the stage and moves across, doing whatever needs to be done, and exits on the other side. No dialogue, no other people. By the behavior, the audience should know where he's entering from, what the area is onstage, and where he's exiting to. In other words, are your choices clear and specific enough to communicate what's beyond?

Talk Mirror. The students play mirror in couples, side-coached into alternating who's the mirror and who's the initiator. After a while, they must also alternate mirroring each other's speech—which is to be spoken at normal speed.

Three-Way Mirror. The students play mirror in threes, side-coached into rotating clockwise who are the mirrors and who's the initiator.

Three-Way Conversation. Three chairs are set up side by side facing the audience. The students in chairs 1 and 3 have silently picked topics they want to have conversations about. When I say go, they both start their separate conversations with the person in chair 2, who has to carry on both conversations simultaneously without ever combining them. No questions are allowed. Everyone in the class has the opportunity to sit in all three chairs, having chosen different topics for when they are in chair 1 and when they are in chair 3.

Entrances and Exits. It's more about giving focus than about getting focus. Four or more people per team plan a scene (Who, What, Where, outer wants, opening emotion) with at least four or five places to enter or exit. There must always be at least two people on-stage. Everyone has to try to make as many entrances and exits as possible. Only one person can enter or exit at a time. However, you can't make an entrance or an exit unless everyone else onstage is

Gilda Radner and Eugene Levy, 1974

Second City alums with Fred Kaz in the center

Dan Aykroyd and Eugene Levy, 1974

Catherine O'Hara and Andrea Martin, 1976

The Early Years Panel during the fortieth-anniversary celebration with Joyce Piven,
Avery Schreiber, Alan Arkin, Sheldon Patinkin, Mina Kolb, Bernie Sahlins, and Robert Klein

Dave Thomas and Catherine O'Hara, 1975

Mina Kolb, Joyce Sloane, Richard Kind, and Jeff Garlin
at the fortieth-anniversary celebration

Martin de Maat

Cast of the revue *Terminal Two,* 1973

Backstage at Second City's fortieth-anniversary celebration with
Jeff Garlin, Harold Ramis, Andrew Alexander, and Peter Murrieta

Martin Short, 1978

Tina Fey and Kevin Dorff at the
fortieth-anniversary celebration

Tina Fey, Tom Gianas, and Tim Kazurinsky
at the fortieth-anniversary celebration

John Candy and Joe Flaherty, 1974

Joe Flaherty and Rachel Dratch at the
fortieth-anniversary celebration

Tim Meadows and Avery Schreiber at the
fortieth-anniversary celebration

Mike Myers, 1987

Marc Hickox and Doug Morency, 1998

David Pasquesi, Bernie Sahlins, and Neil Flynn
at the fortieth-anniversary celebration

A toast to Second City's fortieth anniversary with Ed Furman, Tami Sagher, Stephnie Weir,
Susan Messing, Mick Napier, Kevin Dorff, Rich Talarico, and Andrew Alexander

Don DePollo and Ann Ryerson

Ryan Stiles and Dana Andersen, 1987

Writers Panel Discussion during the fortieth-anniversary celebration with Harold Ramis,
Tim Kazurinsky, Peter Murrieta, Jeff Garlin, Tom Gianas, Adam McKay, Jon Glaser,
Tina Fey, Jenna Jolovitz, and Kevin Dorff

Sheldon Patinkin and Alan Arkin at the
fortieth-anniversary celebration

Lindsey Leese and Colin Mochrie, 1990

The Second City Training Center faculty circa 1991 (from left): Anne Libera,
Michael McCarthy, Fran Adams, Ruby Streak, Carey Goldenberg, Sheldon Patinkin,
Martin de Maat, Frances Callier, Mick Napier, Jim Sherman, Joe Keefe, Don DePollo,
Eric Forsberg, Norm Holly, Roberta Williams, and Ron West

looking at you while you're doing it. Furthermore, you can't announce an exit ("I'm going to get some tea"), and you can't talk offstage to make an entrance. If an entrance or exit is made, and not everyone onstage is looking at you, you have to go back. It's a very hard game, and students usually fail miserably the first time or two they play it.

Preoccupation. Three to five people per team plan a scene (as with Entrances and Exits, inner wants would make things too complicated and would split focus into too many shards). They must make sure the What is very physical and very mutual. (An assembly line, for instance, isn't mutual; each person has a separate job.) They're told they'll all have to participate in the activity throughout the scene. They also have to plan a topic of conversation not related to the physical activity. While doing the scene, they *cannot* talk about the physical activity, although they have to keep talking as well as working throughout. The topic of conversation is something they can start with or fall back on; they don't have to keep to it exclusively. They can talk about anything they want except the activity. (It's therefore best that the wants not be connected to the activity, though the students don't have to know that.) Also a very hard game, it too is prone to first-time failure.

Other than in Bus Stop, during the first classes the students have probably been playing characters close to their own persona. In the third or fourth class, they're told that at least one character they improvise with has to be different from their own public persona. If you usually play high status, play low status; if you're comfortable with your sexuality, play someone who isn't; if you're intelligent, play someone who isn't; and so on. How does that choice affect your physical life as well as your emotional and intellectual life? But whomever you're playing, that person has to like himself and believe he has the right to his wants, or you're likely to wind up playing a caricature instead of a character. (A caricature is here defined as a character that can't change, like Pauly Shore.)

What pretty much every acting teacher is teaching, no matter what system, is what to do and what to think about so you won't be thinking about whether you're doing it well or not. (Face it, that's what playing wants, goals, objectives, whatever you call it, is for.) Of course, all the technical aspects of playing the character have to be ingrained in you before the work goes before an audience. No character is ever thinking about such things as "Am I loud enough?" or "Am I walking or speaking correctly?" or "What's my next line?" It's also anathema to judge your performance while you're doing it ("Boy, that really worked" or "That really sucked").

With each new character you play, you have to learn how that person relates to each of the other characters he meets. We all behave differently with different people and in different situations. How does *this* person behave with a boss? with a lover? with a parent? with a pal? with a stranger? and so on. Does she behave differently with different people onstage with her at the same time? How does her body language change from person to person? (It helps to play improv games as characters you're working on, putting them in situations and even with characters different from those in the script. Many acting techniques are best ingrained by improvising in characters.)

When learning to build characters, you have to examine every aspect of your physical, vocal, and emotional being. It's important that you become totally self-aware, so that you know what's you and what's the character, and which of the two belong together and which don't. It doesn't matter how many of your own characteristics you carry over to any given character, so long as they're by choice, not just because that's what you do. Everything must be by choice.

If you can't *invent* the circumstances that will allow you to reach the emotions needed, if you feed off your own emotional traumas, you've limited your emotional range. (And you'll probably end up in a room with padded walls, which is why I don't have students relive their own personal traumas in class. If you have a teacher who demands that of you, make one up.) The point is, we've all made choices early in our lives, consciously or not, about which emotions we're willing to feel again and which we're not, but are those the same choices your character has made? And, if not, can you invent the circumstances that will allow you to go where he goes?

I assume you know how to speak correctly for each new character— how to pronounce the letter *s*, when to say "get" and when to say "git," all that voice training and accent and dialect stuff. But are you aware of speech patterns you carry with you from character to character? One I get annoyed by is the regular taking of pauses in the middle of a thought or phrase. That means all your characters stop periodically to think about what word to say next. It becomes a mannerism—it certainly did for some of the early Method actors—and not necessarily applicable to every character you play. It also makes some of them dumber than they're meant to be. (All Shakespeare's characters are verbally adept. And you'd better not take any unwritten pauses in Pinter or Mamet, or you'll ruin the speech and probably the play.)

A lot of people build characters off characters they've seen in movies or on TV. Don't. That's already a character, and therefore already a distillation of a real human being, and you'll probably end up with a caricature. You might use that character for a sketch show or a musical revue, where you don't have time during the few minutes the character is onstage to reveal anything but the most obvious personality traits while getting your laughs.

You know how to do it. You already have a lot of characters in you with room for many more: that teacher you were really good at being when that teacher wasn't present, your relatives, your neighbors, your best friends, your worst enemies, some of your classmates. You know them, and in more than one kind of situation. You even understand some of their psychology, how they're likely to respond in various situations. They're good people to build characters off, particularly the physical life, as with animals. And, to keep the mechanism oiled, observe strangers (sneakily, please) while you're on a bus, or standing in line, wherever. Figure out things about them and about how they feel about themselves. Mirror them, if you can do it unobtrusively, please, or after they're out of sight. How do they walk? How do they sit? When do they gesture? How much gesturing do they do? How does mirroring them, including the face, make you feel about yourself? And take psychology courses.

Acting is pretending to be other people; it's "make-believe," as Laurette Taylor, the original Amanda in *The Glass Menagerie,* called it, Stanislavsky's "magic if." When we were kids playing cops and robbers or impersonating the gym teacher, whatever, we were fully committed to playing what we were playing, and it was real for us. We didn't judge ourselves in terms of whether we were doing it well or not, and neither did anyone else. That's what the actor has to get back to. We didn't know there was such a thing as technique, we didn't know there was such a thing as the art of acting; we were playing. (Actually, we were improvising in character.) The actor needs to build her technique strong enough, in class work and during the rehearsal process, so that by performance time, she can go back to just play, like when we were kids. Sure, it's hard. It's harder work than anybody who doesn't do it understands it or can understand it. But it can't look hard. Meryl Streep is an excellent actor, but you do often see that she's "working" in a lot of her films. You never see that in Dustin Hoffman's work. You always do in Barbra Streisand's, calculated to the inch. You never thought Spencer Tracy or Humphrey Bogart—two of my favorite long-ago actors—were working; they were just being, true now of Michelle Pfeiffer and Susan Sarandon.

You're cast in a role because of the similarities the director sees and hears between you and the character. It's then your job, for at least the first half of the rehearsal period, to find the differences, then put back the similarities you may have lost in the process. Building a character is reading the script, paying attention to what's said about your character as well as what your character says, and gradually, both externally and internally, finding that "in you" and that "not in you" that go together to make how you play that character. And how you play that character isn't like how anybody else plays that character. But how you play her is also dependent on and built off how the other actors play their characters. To that extent that, if there's a cast change, it probably won't change the psychology of your character, but it's likely to change how you play any given moment with that new actor. And it should. And hopefully you're free enough and know your character well enough to play each moment as that moment that time. Being together in the moment is, ultimately, the core of everything I teach and direct.

—*Sheldon Patinkin*

AN IMPROVISATIONAL ALMANAC: PART FOUR

Explore each beat to its fullest, then let it go.

❧ ❧ ❧

Playful, direct, codeveloped ideas, information, or dreams will always be far hipper than one person's alone.

❧ ❧ ❧

Everything can be as obvious as a symbol in a dream.

❧ ❧ ❧

For building a machine, go with a different motion than what is already there, and then interconnect with at least two other actions.

❧ ❧ ❧

Try to bring a brick rather than a cathedral to a scene or improv.

❧ ❧ ❧

Think on the laughter; talk and move on the silence.

❧ ❧ ❧

No scene is ever about the words that are being spoken.

❧ ❧ ❧

Always respect your audience. As a group, their intelligence is higher than yours, simply because they have many more minds to draw from, as compared to your five to eight players.

❧ ❧ ❧

There is a wealth of humor available through status differences and the playing thereof. Realize it and play with it. The changes and shifts that are inherent are ripe for the taking.

❧ ❧ ❧

Think of improvisation as worshipful play. In scenes, try to think profoundly and it will come off as pretentious. Profoundness will come out of natural honest exploration of reality.

❧ ❧ ❧

Try not to follow one group activity with another one.

❧ ❧ ❧

We should be rational about our irrationality.

❧ ❧ ❧

If the whole is going to be art, the parts must not strive to be.

❧ ❧ ❧

Improvisation is the ultimate disposable art form. It is like toilet paper; if one sheet isn't working, let it go and try another one. Try not to be tied to any one moment or discovery. One of the most important aspects of the work is to keep the discoveries fresh, and make them new each time, rather than go about the same moment each way in the same way.

❧ ❧ ❧

Onstage the thinking should be in an ecological fashion; nothing should go to waste.

❧ ❧ ❧

If one doesn't play the game, one can become the victim of the game's punishments.

❧ ❧ ❧

Try not to spend too much time and energy building a character; they're already there to be discovered and utilized.

❧ ❧ ❧

Most any common object or attitude can inspire a character: a lemon, a pumpkin, a Ford Bronco, a pencil sharpener. "The world is beautiful" or "Nobody loves me." Using the idea as a seed, let the character evolve to a flower as quickly as possible.

❧ ❧ ❧

Be aware of patterns; play with them.

❧ ❧ ❧

The challenge is to lose control: experiencing mental vertigo, changing "oops" into rarified logic. The discovery of improv is landing in the same place/space, and using it to the best of your ability.

❧ ❧ ❧

There are no minor plays by a player.

❧ ❧ ❧

After an exit, on your entrance, come in with the same attitude and new information.

❧ ❧ ❧

If you are doing a teaching scene, the role of the teacher should keep fading in and out of focus. The teacher should not dominate the scene. The leader of the scene is responsible for bouncing the focus off all the others in the scene.

❧ ❧ ❧

If you go offstage keep your reality going. Visualize your offstage actions, keep real time going, and then come back.

❧ ❧ ❧

Learn to discover human nature instead of what you want the scene to be about.

CHAPTER FIVE: LONG FORMS, SHORT FORMS, SCENES, AND GAMES

Improvisation: The Fine Line between Suck and Not Bad and How to Get Away from That Line and Go to Another Line Where the Options Are Better

There is no one I would rather have as a part of an ensemble than Adam McKay. He has no interest in interpersonal politics—who likes whom, who is in, who is out. His entire concern is the quality of the work at hand and whether everyone is contributing to that quality of work. That concentration and focus rubs off on everyone who works with him. Adam was one of the driving forces behind The Second City long-form show Lois Kaz. *I have never seen a touring company produce as much unique original work as Greenco did when he was a member. His one Mainstage show was the groundbreaking* Piñata Full of Bees, *from which he was hired to write for* Saturday Night Live, *where he quickly became head writer. Did I mention that he is hysterically funny? Adam is also a sincere student of the art of improvisation—in all its forms from games to scenes, long and short.*

"Improvisation," wrote the fourteenth-century philosopher and metallurgist Fredrick Ollenhauer, "is the inhale and exhale of life, common yet miraculous in perpetuity." And though this is a made-up quote, the point is still a valid one. "Improv" or "Impro" or "Makes-'em-ups-as-you-goesalongsies" is an art form so simple and visceral that often people show up for performances with a six-pack or wearing referee shirts. That's pretty raw. So with that in mind, why is it important to talk about theories and forms for a theatrical art that most people relegate to warm-up exercises or party games? The End.

No, wait, I thought of an answer. . . . It's important to talk about it because your first instincts can be sharpened and educated! (That last sentence was to be read kind of loud and out of breath, like a fifteen-year-old discovering a mint copy of *Legion of Super Heroes* number 214 under a stack of *Us* magazines.)

That's right, because if you find a teacher who's good, there are potentially cool and inspiring ways for groups to behave and perform onstage —rules and codes of improvisation that create multilayered and kaleidoscopic meditations on the contradictions of the modern world, rules that if applied to normal life would transform our violent and reactionary world into a world not unlike one of the fantasy sequences from the movie *Brazil*. Have I attended such a performance before? No. Usually it's eight sweaty twenty-four-year-olds trying to learn how to loosen up at the ad agency or trying to meet friends for their frat floor hockey league. But sometimes, if you're very still . . . it gets good. And it gets sharp. Even if it's just for five minutes, you're still watching six or seven people behave really, really well while still being creative. And that's rare.

Totalitarian states get people to act politely but then the art is usually of the Justin Timberlake variety. And the Lower East Side is a great place to go to express yourself freely but then people steal the one unchained wheel of your bike and whip quarters at you while yelling, "Get lost, gentrifying yuppie." So when it comes to seeing the better side of human nature, group improvisation is pretty good. Like a B plus.

Now suddenly the idea of listening and learning in an improv class for a few months on how not to be a hog or a negative black hole gets pretty interesting. And the beauty of improv as opposed to TV, movies, and even scripted theater is that it can't work with hogs and black holes or people who voted for George W. Okay, the George W. knock was gratuitous and sure I've had my hoggish SUV moments onstage but the point is: George W. Bush is a dangerous corporate shill who will lead our country to economic ruin and WWIII. The End.

Obviously not the point or the end. . . . The point is best expressed by about a dozen Del Close quotes. Del was of course a misanthropic pagan improv teacher, who despite himself taught a pure form of selfless Christian improv—stuff like agreement as a natural and powerful state, finding your third and most intelligent thought, overestimating your audiences, and the idea of making others look good as a means to looking good yourself. He also invented dozens of forms for groups to improvise through, each one a very, very loose outline for a potentially stunning long one-act play.

When you've improvised for five or six years and been on groups with names like "Habeas Porpoise" and "Bouquet of Flesh," you have to move on. Because improvisers make zero money. But then all the things you learned apply to everything you do from then on.

All right—I should stop for a second because I just realized I sound like a commercial for why you should pay four hundred dollars for an eight-week improv class. That isn't my point. Don't pay if you can get away with it. Give the teacher your electric bill check and then act like it was an accident. Pretend to slip on the stage and then threaten to sue the theater unless they give you free classes, whatever it takes. Especially at Second City. They just opened their sixth theater in Boca Raton so they've got the cake.

I was going to continue on the idea of improv relating to everything but then even I got bored. So that's it.

—*Adam McKay*

Del Close

You may have seen Dave Pasquesi in small television or film roles—he has appeared as Larry David's dentist on Curb Your Enthusiasm *and as Hank the caterer in* Father of the Bride. *You are probably more familiar with his voice from numerous commercials, including many for McDonald's. Dave has stayed in Chicago and has made a name for himself as a "straight" theater actor, including a critically acclaimed turn as Ricky Roma in a Steppenwolf Theatre Ensemble production of David Mamet's* Glengarry Glen Ross. *He and another Second City alum, T. J. Jagodowski, occasionally perform an intelligent and unique fully improvised two-man show at the theater where Del Close spent his last years teaching—Chicago's ImprovOlympic.*

I will not attempt to tell wild stories of excess. That is not my experience.

I believe them all to be true.

I was the beneficiary of some excellent advice given to a friend of mine. He was told by his brother to seek out Del Close and take his workshops. After a couple of weeks we found this Del fellow on the second floor of a bar/cabaret called CrossCurrents in Chicago. We "auditioned" at the beginning of class and were invited to stay. That was 1984 (I think). I have been trying to be a better improviser since. I did not realize it then, but that was the beginning of learning from Del for the next fifteen years.

I was fortunate to have been introduced to Del after he and Charna Halpern had teamed up. This was after Del had removed some of the bad habits in his personal life that got in the way of his teaching of improvisation.

To my knowledge, until that time, improvisation was mostly short sketches. When Del directed the Committee in San Francisco, they used a way of loosely improvising around a theme introducing ideas and characters, which would be honed into sketches for performance. This long-form, improvisational rehearsal game was nicknamed the Harold. Del wanted to turn this method of developing material in a workshop setting into a performance piece that would be dependable enough to run as a show. We were the group of improvisers who happened to be there for Del to experiment with. Mostly, we showed him what this thing shouldn't look like. One of Del's best lessons was that failure is better than never having tried to succeed. Failure was lauded as long as it was not tentative; tentativeness was unforgivable.

An important ingredient in Del's teaching was that he was an accomplished improviser in his own right. He was a performer: a stand-up, a fire-eater, an improviser, and an actor as well as a director. He was real smart. And so he knew what he was asking of us, and knew it was possible. As a fearless character, he expected us to be fearless to some degree as well. He often thought more of his students' abilities than they did of their own. A stand-out for me is when each of us had to improvise a monologue. When we did, poorly, Del remarked, "That was not very good," and suggested we try it again. "This time, you're all poets. Your words are important." We tried again, and to much greater success. The idea was that we need not fill all the space with words. Cut the tendency to overexplain if you can afford to leave things ambiguous. The importance of working with Del was in these clear yet powerful directions with practical application. Things like: don't dilute the importance of what you say with all those extra words. He was larger than life in reputation and in reality. And . . . he was scary. You did not want Del angry or disappointed. I found I was inspired to please him because I admired the guy. I wanted to be as smart and as dedicated to improvisation as he was—and still do.

We were attempting to create a longer form of improvisation. The response Del was after was not so much laughter as cheers, which is only possible if you withhold the smaller laughs and let them build to something else. One way to make it longer was to slow it down. I believed, incorrectly, that the goal of improvisation was to be fast and funny and talk a lot. I was wrong. There was no need to rush because we were in no hurry. Leave room to think. We didn't have to quickly get to the next laugh.

He often likened performance to a contest or competition. The idea behind it is that there are no heroes without extraordinary tests. Del set up a situation in which we had the opportunity to be heroic.

He was a great teacher and advocate of improvisation. He instilled in me values for improvisation, ideals to reach toward. He made us believe that to become a good improviser was a worthy goal . . . that you didn't have to know what the end of something was going to be before you jumped in wholeheartedly.

I must say that Del may not have taught these things, but I attribute them to him anyway. I have attended classes taught by students of Del who say, "Del said . . ." and then they give a rule of improvisation. I was in class with them. I don't remember Del ever giving a rule. He may have said that there are certain behaviors that tend to prevent the scene from progressing. Everyone in those classes understood the lessons differently. This is how I understand them.

Class would start on Monday evenings with a lecture of sorts. Del would talk about something he was reading (Greek myth, science fiction, a comic book, H. L. Mencken) and we would try to figure out how, or if, it related to improvisation. Then he put us onstage to see how this new information affected us. He didn't pretend to know what was going to happen.

This was another great lesson I learned through observing Del and it is liberating: you aren't supposed to know what is going to happen.

The ideas Del taught me that I try to implement while improvising include the following:

The other people onstage with you are the most important people in your life. They are the answer to all your troubles. Look to them. Listen with all your senses. Listen and pay attention. You can afford to be selfless on stage without the repercussions of the real world.

Always work at the top of your intelligence. All your characters know everything you know. Del gave permission to be exactly as smart as we are—no excuses. If you're playing a hillbilly, that hillbilly is as smart as you are. If you're playing a neurosurgeon, that neurosurgeon is as limited as you are.

Try to skip your first impulse to respond, and move on to the next, less obvious one. This is contrary to most academic advice that the first thought is the best one. It just isn't. Sometimes, it's the third thing you think of.

We were not expected to be funny, but we did have a responsibility to be interesting.

Respond honestly. You can afford to tell the truth onstage. Your honesty will be perceived as "acting." I still remember the first time I got a huge laugh from a simple, honest response. Truthfully, it was not funny to me, nor was it intended to be funny, and yet they laughed. I learned that I should do what I think is right; the audience will make of it what they will.

Don't let your imaginary objects get in your way. Again, the most important thing is the relationship with the other person, not where the pretend cup goes.

Of course there are more lessons than I can recall. These are just a few I have not yet perfected . . . it's plenty to work on. Improvisation is impossible to do perfectly—if you're doing it right. Del taught that these principles cross over into all types of performance. The foundation of good acting is great listening and responding honestly. But with a script, you know the words you're going to use.

Del and I worked together in a couple different shows as actors and I watched him put his teaching into action. This was another lesson, because I knew he could practice what he had preached for those many years. It was practical, usable information—not mere theory.

As a director at Second City, he described his function as pointing out to the actors what it was they were already doing. "That scene in the pickup truck is about gun control," he declared one day. None of us knew that or intended that, but sure enough, it sure did look like that. He was the eyes in the back of the room telling us what was actually being seen from the audience, irrespective of what we wanted to come across.

I have been greatly influenced by Del, mostly for the better. His love for improvisation was undeniable and infectious. And did I mention . . . he was scary.

—*David Pasquesi (Directed by Del Close)*

Producer emeritus Joyce Sloane is well known among The Second City community for never throwing anything away. Her office at the end of the hall is filled with pictures, mementos, and files filled with seemingly every piece of paper ever generated during the theater's forty-plus-year history. While helping Sheldon Patinkin do research for his book The Second City, *I got to dig through some of Joyce's files. I found a bio scrawled by Bill Murray in crayon on the back of a piece of scrap paper and a letter from a college student named Peter Tolan explaining why Second City should hire him. (Peter went on to become a very successful television and film writer, including executive producing* The Larry Sanders Show *and cowriting* Analyze This *with Harold Ramis. He never did work for Second City.) I also found these notes from a workshop on improvisation taught by Del Close in the early 1980s.*

1. *"Yes, and . . ."* This is the fundamental rule of improvisation. "No" is a word that has the effect of stopping the action of a scene. It is the verbal equivalent of upstaging the other actor. Fun for the actor, no fun for the audience.

2. *Progress the action.* For example: "Let's go get those guys!" "No, let's wait."—*wrong*. This should be: "Let's go get those guys!" "Right. I'll go around the back."—*agreement and progression.*

3. *Concentrate on the relationships.* People are more interesting than scenery and props. Conflict is only a small part of a relationship. Events are the result of the interaction of many relationships.

4. *Take the active choice.* Two different choices in a scene may progress the action. Choose the more physical or the one involving the use of the most actors or the greatest effort.

5. *Follow the fear.* This is stage fright. Use the energy of that fear to heighten your performance. It is more interesting to watch a character facing fear than denying fear.

6. *Play against it.* If the scene or action becomes too predictable, do the opposite. This is a positive form of conflict.

7. *Support your fellow actors.* Make the other actor look good, no matter how stupid his or her choice may be in your scene. A "Great idea, let me help!" attitude makes you look good.

8. *Go for your first instinct.* This is the most authentic emotion. Hesitation is negative and slows the action of the scene.

9. *Follow the rule of three (or thirds).* Anything *important* to the scene should be mentioned or seen three times—no more, no less. Awareness, possibility, actuality.

10. *Play up to the intelligence of the character.* This does not mean speaking with an English accent. Your own intelligence is okay. Your character may be a total idiot. Play his achievements, not his failures.

11. *Use the English language.* Take advantage of the possibilities of description in the English language. This also applies to pidgin and jive. Use the rhythm and color of the whole language as opposed to dropping occasional words in an English idiom sentence.

12. *Be specific.* "Look over there!"—*wrong*. "Look on the couch under the blue pillow!"—*correct*.

13. *Use proper names.* Not, "Hey, ah, fella?" but, "Hey, you in the red bowling shirt, 'Lefty,' up with your hands!"

14. *See everything, hear everything, use everything.* Everything said

onstage or appearing onscreen is noticed by the audience. When actors ignore something, it causes a negative reaction in the audience.

15. *Start in the middle of the action.* The active choice, again. Be doing something important instead of doing nothing when the scene opens.

16. *Concentrate on the details.* Details of objects, faces, and gestures are much more revealing and interesting than a succession of master shots. "I love your hat" is not as interesting as "I love that little brown tassel on your cowboy hat!"

17. *State the obvious.* If you vocalize the one obvious fact that everyone is aware of and too embarrassed to mention, it will get a laugh every time.

18. *Be willing to embarrass yourself.* If you are not willing to embarrass yourself onstage, you will never, ever achieve greatness as an actor.

19. *Don't invent; remember.* It is easier to remember a situation than it is to invent one on the spot. Let the right brain do the work. Reality is always stranger than fiction.

20. *Allow ideas to form in the progress of the scene.* Do not go into an improvisation scene with all the beats worked out. Allow time for new ideas to happen. Do not panic when things do not happen when *you* want them to happen.

21. *Understand pattern development.* Be alert in a scene to developing patterns of conversation and action. "The quick brown fox jumped over the . . ." The audience knows what you should say, as well as your fellow performers, so say it.

22. *Silence creates tension.* The improvisational scene onstage or on TV or in a film is *not* a radio show. We need not always overtalk a scene. Action and silence speak louder. Let the audience have time to build their own expectations.

23. *Play a game within the scene.* A game allows characters to become themselves and to develop other parts of their characters. Have a sense of playing a game when playing in a scene. Audiences

enjoy absorbing themselves in the game. This is why TV game shows are so popular.

24. *Take responsibility for your actions in the scene.* If it's your idea, or your goof, you are responsible. Do not try to blame anyone else. Do not propose what you have to retract later. Have disciplined abandon.

25. *The scene ends when the action comes full circle.* When the audience recognizes similarities to the opening action or scene, they think, "This is where I came in!" A completed cycle of life has occurred.

26. *Keep something hidden.* "Well, that's all I know about him, Inspector." Let the audience think you know *more* about him.

27. *Cut before the climax.* This is related to keeping something hidden. It sustains interest. To drag out a scene is to lead audience interest to such a conclusive end that it becomes difficult and often impossible to revive the action and audience interest. They become "drained"; compare the situation to a porno film that shows "too much."

28. *Women are not funny.* Audiences laugh when men are made out to be fools in a scene.

29. *You are always onstage.* The "audition" begins when first contact is made with a director, not when it's scheduled to begin. Keep alert to enter a scene whenever you are needed.

—*Del Close*

Del Close Games

Del Close joined The Second City cast in 1961, leaving the cast in 1964. After spending time in San Francisco, where he worked with the Committee, he returned to Chicago in 1972. Del continued his association with The Second City—working as a director and teacher in Toronto and Chicago on and off through 1989, when he directed The Gods Must Be Lazy. *Throughout his life, Del was constantly innovating. He first developed the long-form impro-*

visational structure the Harold when he was with the Committee. His book
Truth in Comedy *(written with Charna Halpern and Kim "Howard" John-*
son) gives a fairly complete account of the Harold as he developed it at Im-
provOlympic, the theater that David Shepard started with Charna Halpern.
The following reminiscence from Avery Schreiber details some of Del's early
improvisational experiments.

During the years I worked with Del at Second City in Chicago and London
he evidenced a challenging take on what we were striving to do. He came
up with a format that was a precursor to what Paul Sills did in putting the
Story Theater format together . . . a device that called for a narrator and the
creative input of the entire company in an On the Spot improv, based on
the day's news items, with give and take, allowing the scene to grow and
take form differently each time it was played. It followed easily in the path
of Opera improvs I had seen and performed in sets, and we felt it was an
exciting, daring new way to play. I have always admired it as a wonderful
improvisational construct. I have used it in advanced workshops and I call
it Del Narrativo. Here is how it's done:

DEL NARRATIVO: *Number of Players.* A narrator and a team made up of any
number of players

Suggestion. A theme, a newspaper item, or anything that is currently
"hot"—for example, "Presidential Cover-Up"

To Play. The narrator steps forward and begins to tell the story, setting up
Who, What, Where as needed. The team acts out what is said, exploring
and expanding on the scene. The narrator then adds what has been introduced by fellow players, building it into the unfolding version. The rest is
Give and Take as the team and the narrator share the creation of their developing story.

The Game Game/Marienbad

The Game Game, or Marienbad as it used to be known, was invented by
Del Close and John Brent in 1962. The audience does not know that there
are no rules except that the first to claim three points wins. It starts as a

word association game that expands to gestures and sounds made in try-ing to top each other's gambit. At any time a player can capitalize on the others' delay in responding, repetition, or departure from what is an emerging matrix of connectability: to take a point. If the other challenges the point taken you have to have a very good reason to back it up or the point is given to the challenger. In the event that the players become bel-ligerent the person who introduced the game and the players can act as referee . . . and if *they* are challenged it is thrown open to the audience to judge, and the house awards the point.

The best playing of this gets the audience involved and taking sides, even though they don't know what the fuck is going on.

As Del and John played it, it seemed to have no rules; at least, the rules were very obscure. As they played they were always in agreement, includ-ing junctures of apparent conflict, when justification or abstract rationale seemed to become mediating factors as points were given, or taken, in a whimsical, almost Zen, game construct.

I was pleased one night when, at The Second City bar, I saw Del, sad-dened by the fact that Brent was absent and he really wanted to play the Game Game. Bright-eyed and bushy-mustached I quickly offered to play it with him, if he so deigned. Damn if he didn't deign! That night was the first of many, many times we played it, on and offstage, over the years.

One of the devices Del pulled on me became the ending of the game for a while. After admitting being outwitted by me twice in a row his ap-parent anger flashed and he announced, "I win." He turned as if to leave the stage. I was up two points and I challenged him, "How do you win?" He puffed on his cigarette, turned smiling, and said, "I cheat!" He'd won. Lights faded.

—Avery Schreiber

What's Better? Long Form or Short Form?

Mick Napier is a leather-clad, chain-smoking, pool shark iconoclast with an uncanny ability to create a safe, nurturing rehearsal and classroom environ-ment. Mick studied with Martin de Maat at The Second City Training Cen-ter and with Del Close at ImprovOlympic. Along with a number of students and friends, he founded the Annoyance Theater, where the combination of freedom, safety, and a genuine love of the perverse lead to the creation of productions with titles like That Darn Anti-Christ!, Coed Prison Sluts, *and* Hot Monkey Pi. *As a teacher Mick Napier is an astonishing diagnostician— assessing each student's strengths and weaknesses in a matter of moments and offering concrete advice that can immediately be actively put into practice. His journals of his experience while directing The Second City production* Paradigm Lost *were published on the Annoyance Theater Web site and became an instant classic. Mick's advice on being the perfect ensemble member is useful to anyone working in a group—"Never interrupt each other and if you do, apologize." Mick is currently at work on his own book about improvisation.*

When I started improvising at Indiana University, I had never seen improvisation, let alone performed it. A fellow named David MacNerland and I posted an audition notice on the theater bulletin board for an improv troupe named Dubbletaque. We cast a group of people and began to create comedy. Each week, we would write a whole new show, filled with sketch and improvisation, and perform it at a local tavern called The Rathskeller. We didn't know that we weren't supposed to be able to write a whole new show in a week, but our youth and naiveté fueled the process long into the weeknights, rehearsing and writing when we probably should have been studying. Improvisation was improvisation, and writing was writing. That's how I learned, on my own, at Indiana University.

Then I moved to Chicago, and learned something else. I learned that there are different kinds of improvisation. Games were called games back then, but there was another kind of improvisation. There was a thing called "long form." I remember my reaction to first hearing the words *long form.* I thought, My, that sounds like it would be boring. *Form* is so structured, and *long* is so long. It doesn't have the lively and playful feeling of a "game." To me, long form was merely a different way of improvising, not better not worse. Take a single suggestion and improvise for about half an hour. That's long form. As I began to do long-form improvisation, I also learned how fun it is. Sometimes much more fun than to actually watch. It was truly a different way of improvising, bringing back characters and de veloping some narrative along the way. I improvised in many long forms, learned a lot, and made some people laugh along the way. But to me it was *merely* a different way of improvising.

Somewhere along the way, in the past decade, I heard another phrase I hadn't heard before: "short form." I remember my reaction to hearing the words *short form* at an improv festival in Texas. I thought, Short form? Surely they're not talking about games, are they? Yes "they" were. Somewhere along the way, long form had taken on a "not just different," but "a bit better" perception. It had come to be perceived as a more substantial way of improvising, an improvisational method with more integrity than the games. This was propagated not only by the people doing long form, but also the people doing games. Somewhere along the way, in reaction to the perception of "long form," someone created "short form" as a way of justifying the integrity of games. That's when I laughed. The "art" of improvisation is being defined by its length of time: a long one and a short one. Because of what long form is, it has created a reaction such that we must call our games "short forms." Sad day.

That was a sad day for me, because I've only ever thought of improvisation as improvisation, by its very definition. You are onstage and you are making up things as you go, and that's it. Its constructs and forms were always derived from that single truth. I believed (and still do) that nothing is better, only different. Different ways of making things up as you go along. Long form is a way and so were the games. But now, some people felt that their way wasn't a good or smart enough way to improvise, so they reacted to that and called their games "short form." "We're not proud that we're doing games when those other people are doing something important called 'long form.' We have to call it something kinda important like 'short form,' yeah, that's what we'll do, see. . . ." So why does all this make me sad?

At the very heart of improvisation is play. I think no one will dispute that. Play is always the real integrity of improvisation. That's how it really gained momentum in the United States; Viola Spolin wrote a book called *Improvisation for the Theater.* It is a book of games to be used to teach children. It is a book of games. At the heart of improvisation is play. We play games. Games are the integrity of improvisation. Even in long form, we will hear, "Are you playing tonight?" or "Yeah, I found the game in the scene." Play and games are the heart of improvisation, and improvisation is about playing onstage and making it up as you go. That we play in different ways needs no measurement of which is better. That the word *game,* the very essence of improvisation, was embarrassing is what makes me sad.

Is a long form performed in ten minutes a short form? Is a Freeze Tag performed for a half hour a long form? A two-person scene performed in three minutes lives as a scene. How long does it have to be performed for it to become a long form? During a rehearsal process for a Second City Mainstage show, I put a fifteen-minute scene at the top of the second act. Was it a long form? We called it a scene. But I've seen two people improvise a half-hour scene and it was called a long form. I guess it really is the amount of time, but I really don't know what that means. It's all improvisation to me.

As adults, we are so eager to create labels for our "play." It helps us define rightness and factions and schools. As children, though, it's different. Timmy is playing football and Jim is playing army and Susan's playing hide-and-seek. Which is a better quality of play? Is Timmy playing better than Susan? Does Jim's way have more integrity? Playing is playing, and improvisation does not give a damn how you do it. You're having fun or you are not. When the process of improvisation becomes the product of what people are paying to see, it is the play that the audience enjoys, regardless of the structure used to present it.

Which is better, long form or short form? Respect for playing is better, regardless of how you do it. That's what I've always believed, since I was young and naive, back with my college group at Indiana University.

—*Mick Napier*

What Is Long-Form Improvisation?

Del Close once told our class: "I've been doing it for forty years, and I don't know what it is."

—*Rich Talarico*

Some Definitions for Those Who Desire Them

The simplest way to define *long-form improvisation* is an improvised piece that is, well, long. Most long-form improv is at least ten minutes in length and consists of a number of short scenes edited by the performers onstage rather than by a stage manager or other outside source. The individual parts of a long form should be related in some fashion. This could be by a common suggestion or in a more complex manner, with each scene ultimately connecting into a coherent whole. Del Close is popularly understood to be the father of long-form improvisation with his creation of the structure known as the Harold.

Short-form improvisation is generally less than ten minutes long and tends not to contain any internal editing.

Performance games are improvisational structures that follow a set of specific rules or guidelines. Most games contain an element that guarantees a certain amount of success in performance. Some showcase special skills or abilities, as in style parody games. Others contain a built-in comic action as in the popular guessing games (Michael Gellman calls these "victim" games) such as Party Quirks in which the audience enjoys being one up on an improviser who must guess at suggestions provided while he was out of the room.

Ideally, an *improvised scene* is a mini–theatrical piece, character driven and focused on the relationship between those characters, with a beginning, middle, and end.

The tendency is to equate long form with scenic improvisation and short-form with games, but in truth most improvisation exists somewhere along the two continuums. If you wanted to be a true improv geek you could create an axis and identify points on a graph for each piece. At one extreme would be a Harold, scenic long form. At the other would be the short-form games of the sort that *Whose Line Is It Anyway?* relies on. But there would also be long-form games, such as full-length improvised parodies. Short-form scenes are the material out of which Second City crafts its revues. Additionally, some structures can fit almost anywhere depending on how you choose to play them. The classic transformation game Switch, or Freeze Tag, could be played as a scenic long form with transformational editing or as a short, fast-paced game that takes its comic action from freezing players in the midst of suggestive poses and offering one-line jokes.

I'd like to suggest that even the most high-concept games could be made richer and more interesting if played with a scenic bent. I once directed a touring company that created a version of Party Quirks revolving around a historical event. The company's goal was to keep an actual scene going as well as the guessing game—the "victim" not only had to guess at the various quirks but also had to deal with the raised stakes of the historical drama in progress.

Scenic Structure 101

The first five to ten lines of the scene should be exposition. Exposition is the information the audience needs to know in order to appreciate the scene that follows. The exposition is followed by the introduction of the issue of the scene (the premise, the conflict, whatever you choose to call it). This issue is then explored and heightened in the rising action until a point of transformation is reached—this is the climax of the scene. This climax is frequently accompanied by a change in character status. The resolution of the scene allows us to briefly see the effects of the transformation on the characters in the scene. The *out* of the scene is the final line, which signifies a light change or blackout. A *hard out* is a joke line—often the status switch bounces back to status quo or the scene is reframed, giving the audience new information that puts the events of the scene in a new light. A *soft out* ends a scene without a joke—often a soft out will be accompanied by a slow fade of the lights rather than a quick blackout.

The key to improvising full scenes that successfully move through a beginning, middle, and end is twofold. First, keep it simple. Once the issue of the scene has been established, it is important not to judge it or attempt to add on additional or "better" issues while you are improvising. Second, many improvisers tend to back off just before the final moment of transformation is reached; they get stuck cycling through the beat just prior to the climax. Have the courage to recognize that transformation is taking place and allow the events of the scene to change your character and affect their status.

If I were directing a Second City show and I had a scene that didn't work, I would just look at the beginning again. Because if you establish a problem at the beginning, then the ending writes itself. If you want to marry somebody or if you want to impress somebody, either you do it or you don't. That's the ending. It's quite simple.

—*Bernie Sahlins*

Don DePollo

There is a kind of conventional wisdom at Second City that the improviser's improvisers—the ones that the other performers line up against the wall behind the bench to watch in the set, the favorites of the waitresses, the hosts, and the dishwashers—never "make it." Dan Castellaneta is clearly the exception to this rule. When I started working in the box office, Dan was on the Mainstage. Shortly thereafter, he left to appear in a new variety series called The Tracey Ullman Show. *And as every student of modern comedy knows, that show led to the creation of the long-running animated series* The Simp-sons, *for which Dan provides the voice of Homer. Dan was also in one of the earliest Second City ETC productions, a show directed by a small man with large glasses and a penchant for wearing Chicago Cubs paraphernalia—Don DePollo.*

I never really saw Donny perform onstage at The Second City. I only witnessed his abilities on the taped archives of past Second City shows.

Donny was like a psychedelic Peter Lorre on speed. His clawlike hands were constantly animated, deftly adjusting his glasses or one of his raven-like hairs that fell out of place over his ears. Funny that I use the word *raven* in association with Donny because it was one of his most famous bits on The Second City stage.

It's been described before but the bit was Donny popping through the window of The Second City set in a black cloak showing only his head and talonlike hands. He then lit upon the arm of Edgar Allan Poe (played, I believe, by Mert Rich), maniacally eating a cracker and squawking, "Never-more!" I have only seen this bit once, at The Second City twenty-fifth re-union show. And as amazing as that was, it was merely the tip of the iceberg of Donny's unfathomable talent and quicksilver mind.

Sometimes in Donny's apartment I would watch him turn down the sound on the television and fill in the dialogue for everyone on the screen —seamlessly switching from one person to another, supplying each one with hysterical dialogue. If it was videotape, he would hit the fast-forward button and still keep up with the rapid series of pictures flashing across the screen.

In some ways the world moved much too slow for Donny. And many who knew him could attest to the fact that Donny's mind was like a hum-mingbird.

Though he was also my director and a friend, primarily Donny was my first real mentor. Donny was a very popular teacher at The Second City, teaching from his own experience but always with a sense of joy and fun. I never saw him criticize or admonish students for failing. Rather he would point out where they could have seized an opportunity—what great thing they created for themselves and how they stopped just short of improvisational paradise. He opened our minds, encouraged us to take risks, but always kept the level of enthusiasm high.

He was also one of the first professionals who encouraged me and told me I could make it as a comedic actor. I'm grateful that I was fortunate enough to have been one of his many students and many friends. I still miss him.

I remember one time Donny recommended I see a play of the late playwright Larry Shue (*The Foreigner* and *The Nerd*) called *Grandma Duck Is Dead*. Donny told me he knew Larry way back in college and that there was a character in it based on him. It is the part of the drum player who can put himself in hypnotic trances. Although the actor who played Donny did not look like him—he was even African American—it was Donny to a T. In that way, I take consolation that Donny DePollo lives on. Somewhere that play is being done and Donny DePollo lives again.

But even more important, shortly after I heard that Donny had passed away after years of suffering and struggling with Crohn's disease, I had a dream where I saw Donny. He was in a basement, dressed in a black cloak and wearing a large beret performing for a group of children who sat in a semicircle around him laughing, amazed at his funny characters and far-out stories. He turned to me and said, "I'm okay, Danny boy. I'm okay." In that sense I know that Donny lives on because of the many people he influenced in his short but amazing life.

—*Dan Castellaneta*

During the summer of 1995, Don was invited to throw out the first pitch at a Cubs game. For Don, whose interest in improvisation was matched only by a passion for baseball (in particular the Chicago Cubs and the St. Louis Cardinals), this was a dream come true. The Chicago Training Center has a small cabaret space on the fourth floor of Piper's Alley that we named (courtesy of Scott Allman) "Donny's Skybox."

Don DePollo was the first teacher many students had at The Second City Training Center. I remember watching a lot of those classes, and almost immediately Donny would have everyone onstage playing one of the million performance games that Don had filed away in his incredibly sharp comedic brain.

Top Ten Performance Games of The Second City National Touring Company

The job of The Second City National Touring Company involves playing to a wide variety of audiences in an array of situations—rowdy college auditorium performances sponsored by the student activities committee, family audiences at midwestern performing arts centers in restored old movie houses, "run out" gigs played in hotel ballrooms for local business holiday parties full of tipsy salespeople, and tours in which the audience's first language isn't even English—as in recent trips to the Far East or the biannual visit to the English Theatre in Vienna, Austria.

Touring Company shows consist of what we refer to as "best of" material—a combination of original sketches with some of the best scenes from the past forty-some-odd years of revues. But audiences don't just come to see the sketches; they come to see the improvisation for which Second City is famous, and unlike the resident company shows where the improv sets are free and the audience is mostly forgiving of failure, the Touring Company performances include a large portion of improvisation as a part of the running order for an audience that expects to laugh.

The performance games that follow are not necessarily the best or most interesting performance games ever created. But they are the games to which the touring companies and their directors return time after time. These are the games that play just as well in front of American college students as they do before a well-dressed crowd of Austrians. These games allow improvisers to show off their wit, their skills, and their reference level. They are games that have built-in gimmicks to provide consistent laughs. And for sheer audience enjoyment there is nothing better than a well-improvised performance game.

CONDUCTED STORY WITH STYLES: Conducted Story is one of those amazing classic Spolin-based games that can be played on a variety of levels of sophistication and expertise. You might not think it, but this game makes a great show closer; it brings the entire cast back together onstage and provides a nice sense of closure to the audience.

Number of Players. Five or six, with a conductor

Suggestions. Each player gets an author, a genre, or "something written on the printed page" (such as a phone book or a cereal box). The conductor gets "the title of a story that has never been told before." A possible additional suggestion is an object that will appear at some point in the story.

To Play. The conductor points to the players in turn; each player must continue the story in his or her style until the conductor points to another player. The more that players strive to tell an actual story as well as show off their skill in mimicking their appointed style, the better. If you're doing a thematic show, you can frame the conducted story as a "bedtime story" or a "Christmas story."

Variation—Conducted Radio. Each player gets a radio station type and the conductor moves up and down the dial.

TAKE THAT BACK/NEW CHOICE: This is a relatively new favorite for our Touring Company shows. It works equally well as a classroom exercise designed to help students move past cliché ideas into more interesting choices and as an energetic justification-based performance game.

Number of Players. Two or three, with a caller

Suggestion. Location, relationship, or historical era

To Play. Players begin a scene using the suggestion. At any point in the scene, the caller will stop the action (often using a bell) and force the player who just spoke to "take back" the previous line and substitute a new choice—or several new choices.

> Example: I love you. [*ding*]
> I hate you. [*ding*]
> I just ate a chimpanzee.

The scene must continue, with all players justifying the final choice.

LOVE LETTERS: This game, in which you ask the audience to fill in the blanks, generally has no official introduction and thus works best later in the show, once the audience has become used to providing suggestions.

Number of Players. Two

To Play. Two characters take turns "writing" each other letters. At various points each player will pause as if at a loss for words and wait until the audience supplies the needed word. Players continue, justifying and expanding on each audience suggestion. There are a number of interesting ways to frame this game stylistically—for example, an ETC spoof of the play *Our Town* included George Gibbs and Emily Webb writing each other letters. The "lovers" could also be competing Civil War generals.

PANEL OF EXPERTS: Audiences love this combination of character-based humor and players' ability to access their reference level.

Number of Players. Five or six, plus a host

Suggestions. Each player is given a field in which they are to be an expert. There are a number of ways to get these fields, depending on the audience and the knowledge of the various improvisers—magazine titles, Olympic sports, foreign countries, and so on.

To Play. The host introduces the panel, often as a talk show of some sort. (When the Touring Company recently played at the English Theatre in Vienna, Austria, Al Samuels would introduce himself as a popular female Viennese talk show hostess and then proceeded to host the game straight as himself. The Austrians found this hilarious.) The host generally asks the first question of the panel and then fields questions from the audience. It can be interesting to frame this game with some sort of theme—a political talk show with unusual guests or sports talk with writers from magazines unlikely to have sports columns.

SWITCH/FREEZE TAG: The classic transformation game that ended almost every improv set for years.

Number of Players. Usually the full cast (for us that's generally six). Can be played with more.

Suggestion. Opening line of dialogue—"Something that you said or wish you had said to someone today"

To Play. Two players begin a scene; the rest form a back line. At some point during the scene, one of the players in the back yells, "Freeze," taps out one player, takes his or her exact physical position, and initiates a new scene, completely transforming the physical position.

STYLE OPTION/OPEN OPTION: This is a great performance game to display both the players' scenic abilities and their skill in genre work. If the audience is very rowdy or seems inclined to shout out "porn" nonstop (although almost every audience will shout out "porn" if given half a chance), the caller can have a little more control by taking a list of genre suggestions while introducing the game and then picking and choosing styles as the game progresses.

Number of Players. Two or three, with a caller

Suggestion. A location, one that can fit on the stage

To Play. Players begin a scene; at various points in the scene the caller will freeze the action and then come to the audience for theater, film, or musical styles. The players will then continue the scene in the chosen style. In Open Option, the caller may ask for a variety of things including emotions, secrets, and hidden information as well as styles.

SCENE TAG: This more scenic version of Switch is not as high energy, but allows for more detailed scene work.

Number of Players. Six to nine, divided into three groups

Suggestions. Each group gets a simple suggestion for their scene (location, relationship, historical era). The first scene also gets an opening line of dialogue.

To Play. The first group or pair begins a scene; at some point during the scene one of the other groups will edit (usually by clapping or calling "Freeze"). That group's scene then replaces the first scene using the last line of dialogue said as the first line of their scene. As play continues, the scenes return—usually with some scenic time having passed between each appearance. A nice way to end this game is with each scene editing in on one line that works differently within the contexts of each of the three scenes.

Editing and Beats

A beat of a scene is the shortest section of a scene that could be a scene by itself. A beat begins with some new action, emotion, or piece of information that is then explored and heightened until it transforms into something else. The end of the beat is that moment of transformation—the point at which the knife is raised, ready to strike.

When editing from the back line or when calling a game, it is always best to edit on that moment of transformation. Watch for when the audience laughs—laughter often accompanies the end of a beat in a comic scene. Good editing is the joint responsibility of all players. The player doing the editing is responsible for watching for and editing on the end of a beat, and the players improvising are responsible for exploring and heightening so that moments of transformation occur.

TIME DASH/EVENT GAME: This long-form game tells a nonlinear story through a series of scenes.

Number of Players. Five or more

Suggestion. An event—for example, the birth of a child or the eruption of a volcano

To Play. Players form a back line as in Switch. Two or more players step out to begin a scene, announcing where they are in time with reference to the event—say, "Two weeks before the surprise party" or "Three weeks after the surprise party." Scenes are edited by members of the back line with each new scene elaborating and building the story of what led up to, and what resulted from, this event. Some versions of this game begin with showing the actual event; I prefer to build toward and ideally finish with showing the event.

ONE-MINUTE MUSICALS: Musical games are a great way to add variety to a show and to showcase the skills of the performers.

Number of Players. Six or more, divided into groups

Suggestion. As in Scene Tag, each group is given a simple suggestion such as a location or relationship.

To Play. Groups come forward one at a time and begin their scene heightening as they go, until the musical director leads in with a musical style. The scene continues but in song. Once the song is completed, the next group steps forward.

Variations. Musical Switch is played just like the classic game except that all scenes are sung (they may include a few lines of spoken dialogue as setup). In Musical Option, the audience provides the style of music and players must continue what they were going to say within the song style.

PARTY QUIRKS/PHRASE: These guessing games all stem from Spolin's Who Am I? game. They are very popular with audiences, and although not officially long form, they can sometimes last ten minutes or more depending on the skills of the guesser or his or her willingness to milk the game.

Number of Players. Five, plus a party host

Suggestions. The host is sent out of the room and each remaining player is given a "quirk," such as "She's two inches tall" or "He's a contact lens" or "He's Madonna."

To Play. Once all suggestions have been given, the host comes back into the room and sets up his party. Guests enter one at a time and the host attempts to guess their quirk while maintaining the party and at least some scenic integrity. Once a quirk is guessed correctly, that player finds a reason to leave. The game ends when all quirks are guessed.

Variations. In Phrase, the suggestion is a common phrase or slogan such as "A bird in the hand is worth two in the bush" (a location for the scene is also taken). Players use the scene to help the guesser come up with the suggested phrase without themselves using any of the words within the phrase. Several other variations include a mock debate with two opponents attempting to guess their topic, and an interrogation in which the criminal must guess his crime.

AN IMPROVISATIONAL ALMANAC: PART FIVE

What you are doing is justifying your existence in the Where.

❖ ❖ ❖

Try to play out and fulfill the moment to its end before you go on to the next.

❖ ❖ ❖

The best way to find something is not to look for it.

❖ ❖ ❖

Do not attempt to parody anything unless you know what, where, how, why, who, and which you are parodying.

❖ ❖ ❖

Treat absurd notions seriously.

❖ ❖ ❖

Comedy can come from seeing a union out of two apparently disparate thoughts/images.

❖ ❖ ❖

One old lady breaks her leg and it is sad. Two old ladies breaking their legs is strange. Three old ladies breaking their legs is starting to get funny.

❖ ❖ ❖

Always be sensitive, be aware, and respond to anyone entering the space or scene.

❖ ❖ ❖

In improvisation, it is not a matter of setting out to "make things," but of letting the improvisation determine what it will become.

❖ ❖ ❖

Don't complicate the complications.

⟿ ⟿ ⟿

On becoming an object, visualize the object by becoming the object.

⟿ ⟿ ⟿

Do unto others as you would have them do unto you. Respect your other actors because in improv what goes around comes around. Remember, they
can turn you into an ashtray, toad, or anything else anytime they want to.

⟿ ⟿ ⟿

If you bring forth what is inside you, what is inside you will save you. If you
do not bring forth what is inside you, what is inside you will destroy you.

⟿ ⟿ ⟿

Every scene is whole; it is only incomplete on another level.

⟿ ⟿ ⟿

To look normal onstage, you have to expend some energy. This level of
performance should be your neutral character. This persona is good for
straight roles, interviewers, and supporting roles.

⟿ ⟿ ⟿

Don't worry about mundaneness. Any scene we start on a mundane level,
by doing what we do, will no longer be mundane.

⟿ ⟿ ⟿

Try not to top somebody until you have equaled them.

⟿ ⟿ ⟿

Keep pulling on the string of ideas—something will take shape.

⟿ ⟿ ⟿

You do not describe your function onstage; the group in the scene decides
your function for you.

⟿ ⟿ ⟿

Explore your Where by handling objects (not props) and reacting to the
discoveries.

⟿ ⟿ ⟿

If something seems like the obvious thing to do, you probably shouldn't do
it. But if it seems like the normally weird thing to be doing, do it.

⟿ ⟿ ⟿

Identify an object. Let the audience know what "it" is. Then you can use the exposition and say, instead of, "Look at the car," "Look at the '55 Thunderbird."

❧ ❧ ❧

Improvisation is a series of choices; you may not be able to choose the situation in which you make your choices, but you are free to choose and think with your response to the situation.

❧ ❧ ❧

Self-consciousness can destroy your thinking; let the audience watch you.

❧ ❧ ❧

Satire dignifies the object by recognizing it; comedy enhances the recognition.

❧ ❧ ❧

Make accidents work.

❧ ❧ ❧

What we are dealing with is a theater in which every decision is ecological and holistic.

❧ ❧ ❧

The lowest level of humor is social satire, the middle level is thinly veiled allegory, and the upper level is high fantasy.

❧ ❧ ❧

Bring the energy of your life to your work; don't suck the energy of your work into your lives. Ground that energy; return it to the earth and the muses whence it came.

❧ ❧ ❧

Make the strange familiar and the familiar strange.

❧ ❧ ❧

A scene is an idea and a comment.

❧ ❧ ❧

Follow the process and the product will follow.

❧ ❧ ❧

When the original idea or moment starts to repeat itself, realize that the circle has completed itself and the scene is over.

⊸ ⊸ ⊸

In group scenes, introduce each character one at a time. Let everyone have their moment. This will allow the audience and the other players to know who is who and what is what.

⊸ ⊸ ⊸

Harolds are like holographs or Etch-A-Sketches: the more we add to them, the clearer they become.

⊸ ⊸ ⊸

When taking suggestions from the audience, try to put them at ease. It is not a test, nor are they on the spot. Define clearly what it is that you want and give a couple of good examples. Encourage them to be creative and at the top of their intelligence.

⊸ ⊸ ⊸

The less you plan, the more you will discover, and the more you plan, the less you will discover.

CHAPTER SIX: **CREATING MATERIAL**

Every time we'd be improvising, they'd say, "Stop writing." I couldn't resist it because you'd be improvising and the person you might be improvising with would go off on some idiotic tangent that you couldn't imagine. You knew what you wanted them to say. It was almost like the Password game where you say, "You're the . . ." and you want them to say "doctor" but they're going to turn out to be the Martian. I couldn't psychically influence what was going on onstage. I love the process of improv, but as soon as I had the opportunity, I started writing down what everyone else was going to say.

—*Harold Ramis*

Doing It Again

An enormous number of successful writers working in the film and television industry got their start as performers at The Second City. It may be that there is something about the process that Second City uses to create material that creates writers. My own pet theory is that blocked writers are drawn to improvisation as a means of forcing themselves to create. After all, you can't stop the scene and play Minesweeper when you're in front of an audience.

Tina Fey was promoted from the Touring Company directly to the Chicago Mainstage when Adam McKay left the company to join the writing staff of Saturday Night Live. *Her work at Second City was notable for her ability to satirize women of a particularly American sort—from the intelligent first lady forced to talk about cookies rather than issues to the "dancer" who strips to CNN and the Boston mother who informs her daughter that "no single item of clothing should cost more than twelve dollars." Tina followed in Adam's footsteps, leaving the Mainstage to write for* Saturday Night Live *and then to serve as head writer—the first female head writer in the history of the show.*

One of the hardest things I ever had to learn at Second City was how to "reimprovise" a scene. It's something you don't learn in class. Then one day you're in a company for the first time and the director says, "Let's put that scene in the set tonight and reimprovise it."

You go onstage and you start the scene the same way you did the night before. You try to remember what lines got laughs and cram those lines in again. Inevitably, they are not funny the second time around. The scene feels flat and forced. You feel like a dirty whore. You're going against everything you've ever learned about improvisation. You're not supposed to know what you're going to say before you go out there. You're not supposed to be setting each other up for bits you've done before. But then, with a few weeks' practice and the desperate panic that you won't have anything in the show, you start to figure it out.

The "game" of what you're being asked to do is not to remember exactly what you did the night before and repeat it. It's more like a video game. If you're playing *GoldenEye 007* on Nintendo 64,* you know you have to hit certain beats of the game to stay alive (shut down a Russian missile system, stop a speeding train), but in between those moments you have a bunch of different corridors and chambers you can go into and sometimes you find a new clue or a treasure or a weapon in there. On the other hand, sometimes you get killed in there. That's what it's like developing a scene in front of an audience.

In the "old-style" Second City sets, the cast would take suggestions from the audience, then take a ten-minute break and go backstage and decide how they were going to use each suggestion. This never worked for the cast I was in. We were too used to Harolds. We thought if we took that break, the audience wouldn't believe we were improvising. And because we didn't believe we were truly improvising, we stunk it up pretty bad.

---

*I feel very confident that this reference will be fresh and appropriate forever.

The way we structured most of our sets was with what we called the Jim Game, which I assume was invented by Jim Zulevic. We would take audience suggestions and write them on a large pad of paper, then stay onstage and use them one or two at a time. "Let's see a scene about abortion and Scooby Doo." Ah, the countless scenes we did about abortion and Scooby Doo. Those were heady days.

Scenes created in front of an audience this way are made of moments more than setups and jokes. If you sit at the computer to write a scene, you might end up with a long, draggy section that doesn't work. But you'll intellectualize that it does work. That part is absolutely integral to the scene! And if those actors won't do it, then fuck them! What do they know about writing?! If you're developing a scene through improvisation, you'll get rid of that section instinctively because you're the one out there with the warm sticky egg on your face.

I'm always surprised when I meet someone who thinks that sitting and writing is the only way of creating comedy. It's like meeting someone who thinks that in vitro fertilization is the only way to make a baby. You want to say, "No, there's this whole other way of doing it that's natural and sometimes pleasurable."

—*Tina Fey*

THE JIM GAME: Tina Fey's assumption is correct; Jim Zulevic created the Jim Game while he was performing at Second City Northwest, the now-defunct location in the suburbs of Chicago. Originally, the idea behind the game was to use up any leftover suggestions that had not been used in the creation of that night's scenes. It was played as a substitute for Switch as a way of ending an improv set on a high-energy note. The idea was not necessarily to create material—it was to use as many suggestions as possible.

To Play. The game is played pretty much as Tina describes it in her essay; the pad is brought out and the unused suggestions are called out—usually two at a time, often the more incongruous the pair, the better. Scenes last anywhere from fifteen seconds to several minutes and may be edited by a player onstage or by the lights.

The Jim Game is now often referred to as a Pad Set, and for some companies it has almost entirely eclipsed the more traditional planned Second City set.

The popularity of long-form improvisation has created something of a vogue for completely spontaneous scene work, scenes in which the participants begin with nothing more than a brief suggestion and come to agreement on the elements of the scene as they go along. Recently Alan Arkin came to the Chicago theater to lead a series of workshops. During the workshop with the touring companies a lively debate developed, with many of the actors insisting that improvising without a plan was a more highly evolved method of improvising; as Tina says in the previous essay, they felt that if they had a plan they weren't truly improvising. Alan held that the method of the scene was less important than the content of the scene—you can improvise a scene without a plan, just as you can build your own parachute while in free fall. It's possible, it's certainly exciting, but it doesn't make the jump any better or more beautiful.

Regardless of where you come down on the issue of pre-planning, if you are using improvisation to create material you will eventually have to

Some Useful Terms

Premise. A one-sentence-long idea for the scene. It could almost function as the title of the scene. It can be simple—"The world's worst blind date"—or more complicated—"Gore and Bush debate as high school students." One good way for improvisers to think about premise is that it is Who, What, Where plus something that raises the stakes. Occasionally the thing that raises the stakes is the point of view. A premise starts the scene but does not dictate what happens in the scene.

Point of View. What the scene is saying; in high school English terms, the theme. Your point of view can be satiric ("The current political system is corrupt") or silly ("It's really funny when we play redneck truckers"), depending on the premise. Point of view is the "truth" in the scene. So if it's *not* really funny when we play redneck truckers, it's going to be a difficult scene to watch or to improvise. You should be able to state your point of view in one sentence or less.

use some of the elements of the planning process, either to flesh out an idea that emerged during a spontaneous improvisation or to create a piece with a more complicated or satiric point of view. I must admit a bit of bias of my own for planned scenes, perhaps because that's what my own training emphasized. But when done well, a planned scene can cut to the heart of an idea or relationship more quickly and more deeply than a cold spot improvisation.

Pre-Planning a Second City Scene

Planning a Scene

Remember that the entire point of planning is to make the scene easier and more interesting to play and watch. If planning certain elements tends to get in your way, don't plan those elements. As you plan you may find that possible actions for the scene begin to write themselves in your head. Try to avoid forcing these actions into the scene as you improvise. Use the planning as the springboard—do the jumping while in the scene.

It can be useful to plan:

The premise

The point of view

The style

The relationship

The location

Brief exposition

Moment before

Individual performers may find it helpful to plan:

Character

Character wants and objectives (as Sheldon Patinkin would say, not just what you want but why you want it)

Secrets

It is generally not useful to plan:

Dialogue beyond a few sentences of exposition

The action

The comic action (unless clearly dictated by the premise)

The "out" of the scene

Jokes for the scene

The Process

Roughly, this is how the process of putting a scene together works.

1. We generate the idea, either through a spot improvisation or discussion.

2. We improvise on that idea. Then we make notes on the improvisation.

3. We improvise again (it inevitably sucks—do not despair). We make more notes.

4. We either improvise again or we script the scene—transcribe it, beat it out, or write it (see the following).

5. We look at the scene as a "written" script. What's redundant or extraneous? What's a good joke we can insert here?

6. We run the scene in the show once or even twice and then review the script.

7. We look at the scene from an acting and directing viewpoint.

8. The scene is now done. It may at this point be altered or cut into parts by the director in order to support thematic or running order concerns of the finished show.

Reimprovising

This is the awkward place between the brilliant original first improvisation and a working written or semiwritten scene. I have found that the best way to reimprovise is to adjust the original planning but to make no attempt to follow any of the action, comic action, or dialogue of the original scene. We have (ideally on tape) the original scene; we are now mining for additional

Action. What happens in the scene. This is what you improvise. A premise may have many different possible actions.

Comic Action. The primary source of humor in the scene. The comic action of *Saturday Night Live*'s Ambiguously Gay Duo is in phallic symbols and homosexual innuendo. A number of improv games like Backward Scene or Dr. Know-It-All have an inherent comic action, which is why they function so well for beginning improvisers. You may go into an improvisation with a rough sense of what that comic action will be or you may find it while you improvise. Certain premises will dictate the comic action.

The videotape quality was so bad when I was here that it would be like six figures of death moving around the stage. They were too cheap to pop for a new camera so I started audiotaping the sets. That was my contribution. By audiotaping the sets, I had a better idea. [We] would do a scene and then my crew was always like "No, no, don't write it. Don't write it, we'll just improvise it." They would improvise *way* beyond where they should've gone. The editing process, they didn't know. I remember I would go back and I'd listen to the eight times the scene was done. I would go "about right there, about the third time . . ." and I would type that up. After the scene was kicked out of the show because it didn't work anymore, I'd say, "It worked when it was like this." It wasn't really writing, it was capturing it when the scene was ready and done. What you learn here—besides timing and when the jokes work and the dying fall and all that—is the editing process.

—*Tim Kazurinsky*

gold to use in our eventual written scene. If you feel that you have all the material you need from the original improvisation, there is no need to improvise more—go ahead and write the scene. In my opinion, the major source of what we at Second City call "second-time blues" is when performers are not really improvising but just trying both to remember the original beats of the scene and make adjustments while on their feet.

Writing a Scene

There are several ways to go about "writing" a scene:

Beat it out. Decide/write out the order of the events of the scene. For example, in the first beat, we establish that there are two very white-bread couples having dinner together in suburbia; in the second beat, we discover that one couple are zombies. The dialogue of the scene is still loose and improvised although certain successful jokes or important lines may be positioned within a beat. Many Second City scenes never get beyond this stage until someone transcribes the show for use by understudies and touring companies.

Transcribing. Someone sits down with a video or audiotape of the scene and transcribes it word for word.

Writing the scene. The scene is written from memory, often incorporating information from several versions of the scene as well as notes and discussion of the improvisations. The "written" version of a scene may differ quite drastically from the original.

The Ensemble Creates a Revue

The process of writing through improvisation is almost by definition a group process. The particular director, cast, musical director, stage manager—what Peter Grosz calls "the ensemble blob"—determines the process of each show, and ultimately the writing process of each individual show is thus a little different from every other. I sat down with the cast of The Second City ETC's Curious George Goes to War *about two months into the run of the critically acclaimed production to talk about the experience of writing that show. Three members of the company—Samantha Albert, Andy Cobb (who had to join the conversation midway through), and Keegan-Michael Key had worked together in the previous ETC show* Holy War, Batman! *Nyima Funk (whose husband, Josh, directed* Holy War*) had just completed a run on the Mainstage in* Embryos on Ice *before joining the ETC cast. For Jean Augustyn and Peter Grosz this was their first experience in writing a show for a Second City resident company. Stage manager Klaus Schuller (who has also directed for The Second City) was able to participate in the discussion intermittently as he came through the green room doing prep for that evening's performance.*

JEAN AUGUSTYN: Right after we opened [*Curious George Goes to War*], our first three or four sets were amazing. It was so wonderful and rich and beautiful. We weren't trying to create material anymore but we were playing with each other like "Whoopee!"

PETER GROSZ: It was like the Shawshank set.

ANNE: Why is it different when you're improvising to create material?

JEAN: I listened to everything I said and judged it. Every time I opened my mouth, and said, "There's a table," I thought with a sigh, That's gonna be in the show. I had no concept of just being in that scene in that moment. It was very, very hard to remove that.

SAM ALBERT: It's the whole idea of moment to moment, which I think makes for the best improvisation and that's what I really admire in how Jean and Peter improvise; they just come in and take a journey with the other person. Nobody really steers; you're sitting in a boat together. I found when it came to creating material that I was definitely trying to steer things into either a point or a showcase or a this or a that. There was a desperation behind creation that is totally the antithesis of what makes good improvisation and what makes good material. That desperation—that "This has to mean something! Can it mean something when repeated Thursday through Sunday until the close?"

PETER: I think we're very fortunate to have videotape and assistant directors. I think you have the luxury of being able to just go reimprovise that scene; you don't have to say all the lines because you already have it on tape from the night before and you already have all these things written down. That whole squashing machine that we came up with in rehearsal where we've got a couple of versions of these scenes and somebody just coalesces them all into this order. It's like each scene achieves its own thing and sometimes each scene sucks in its certain way. You get to take all the sucky parts out and put all the great parts into one scene. It works because you don't have to worry, "Oh, I forgot to say that one funny line about your hat," because you have it on tape.

JEAN: It's also what I like about Second City; it's not only important to be a good improviser but an actor. It helps with reimprovising because you're kind of coming at it like you do in acting class as if it were the first time you were doing it. You can sustain the repetition because you're coming at it from an acting standpoint, not just from a writerly mindset.

ANNE: When do you stop improvising and start acting? Granted, you should be doing both, but when do you make the switch?

JEAN: I think you stop making discoveries—I mean as an actor you still need to make discoveries, but as an improviser you are really establishing when you're making discoveries, and I think once those things are set, in my opinion, then you begin to act because then you have to create the discovery rather than just say, "A wooden leg!"

ANNE: I know there are Second City actors who never stopped improvising. The scenes were never static because they were continually being rewritten.

NYIMA FUNK: There's a difference between changing a line and finding the truth in the line every time you say it. I think the audience needs that or they fall asleep. They need to see that you're actually making this connection with someone. It's Jean that I'm talking to—nobody but Jean—anybody else in her place in this scene, it's a different scene.

PETER: Every show undergoes a certain process of change after it opens. Ideally on opening night we know that most of this stuff is going to work. I'm sure that everybody has thought, I want to change this line, but it's a choice of the building that it's set at opening.

KEEGAN-MICHAEL KEY: Some directors will have a mandate. Some will say, "Just say what you're gonna say because opening night, boobidy-boop, waah, that's it, you're set." And then other directors will say, "Each one of you gets one f-word—use it wisely." And then others, "We're gonna flow into it. We're set, guys, but we're gonna flow into it. Let's feel free while we're doing it but if something's working, please don't take it out just for the sake of change."

NYIMA: I think it's on the director to leave us with a show that can handle change if it needs it. Which means, if you change something the night before opening and you shouldn't have changed it, it's not fair to leave us with a fucked-up line just because you had an idea.

KEEGAN: We don't get to do text analysis. Actually, now that I say it, that's not true. We do text analysis. We do on-the-fly impromptu text analysis. You do it as you write it.

JEAN: I think we should do more. We are responsible for what we say. If we're going to make political statements and care about our work, hell yeah, it's awful to have somebody else come up and say, "Uh, why is that character ordering a Subway sandwich? She's dead." And be like, "Yeah, well, we didn't really care about that."

[Note: Jean is referring to the first-act closer in which Sam Albert is a new employee at a business who is "sacrificed" to the office god—the copier. In "Subway," the patter song that opens the second act, she plays the same character trying to order her lunch.]

PETER: We should be looking at our material. I have a friend who was putting together a demo for an album. He was really obsessing over it, and it was at the same time we were writing the show so we were talking. I was listening to the album and stuff with him and he came and saw the show a couple of times. We were drawing parallels and he said, "You should be able to ask really detailed questions of great works of art." He loves Proust and he thinks you can ask a million different questions of Proust: "Why did you do this? Why did you put this here? Why did your character do this?" And it's all intentional and that's what he really likes. We shouldn't have holes in our show that a person off the street could come and say, "Did you realize that you're having a dead human being, chronologically, ordering a sandwich?"

KEEGAN: Notice how much a callback resonates with the audience—that means they're paying attention.

JEAN: When you tour and you go through the old scenes, you notice the ones that are honed when they are written. Not overindicated or whatever, just there and clean and beautiful. When you pick up a script like that you get it, you can do it, you don't need someone to say, "There's a giant tube of toothpaste behind you. That's why it's funny." You read it and you get it.

ANNE: What does the perfect director do?

NYIMA: Keep your cool. That's a big thing for me. You gotta keep your cool because you're showing us all how to do it and if we see a director crying about something—I remember one of the first directors I had in Detroit for a workshop production, she cried because she didn't have the room she wanted to use. That's a little thing but it's also like, "Fuck you. Now you're gonna tell me what to do in this scene?" You have to be the person that's leading everybody. That's what you're hired to do. Make a decision. Make a choice. I think that's a big thing for me.

KEEGAN: When the director is steadfast on what their process is. When the director can come forward and say, "Okay, here's what we're gonna do for the first four weeks. Then week five and week six, we're gonna do something like this and then when we open the show, it will be set. I will do everything in my power to make sure it's gonna be set. Hopefully, you guys can have two or three days before we open without any RO [running order] changes." It destroys any argumentative strife. Because you can argue if you want, but the other eight people will be looking at you saying, "Do you remember that first day when he or she said blah, blah or this and that? Be quiet and work." One of the other big things is, physically doing things a lot. Ten percent analysis, 90 percent do. Do, do, do, do. When you walk in the door there should be a big, fat poster on the back wall that says NIKE. And everybody should know exactly what that means and then just shut up and do it.

JEAN: I would say put your ego aside enough to let the actors do their thing and try to really understand what that thing is too, so that you don't lose your power or your show to someone who's needy and crazy. Set boundaries, like a healthy relationship. "This is what we're gonna do. This is how we're gonna behave in rehearsal and this is what's going to happen and this is why you'll be safe and allowed to fail."

KLAUS SCHULLER: I really like observing somebody who processes a script. They can take a scene that's being worked on and distill it to its essence. To be able to see repetition and remove beats. Make sure the structure of the scene is intact and boil the scenes down to what they need to have, compacting five minutes into three and that three is so good. That's an editor's skill I love a director to have.

SAM: I have a question actually. This is where I get confused. In terms of writing a show and being an ensemble, what are our roles based on?

Sometimes I think, Yes, we should all be complete transformational performers with a wide range of ability to play different characters and have different points of view. Then I think, But we're an ensemble. If we look at the ensemble as a whole, do we all fulfill a little piece of the pie in that Trivial Pursuit thing where it's like you're the clown, you're the intellect, you're the this, you're the that?

PETER: I think the second part is true and the first part is true because it's not like the circle of the ensemble stays the same, and if there's no crazy girl who has funny eyes then one of you has to be that girl. It's an amorphous ensemble blob. Once everybody comes to it, it sets itself, we all do our own little thing and that makes the shape I think of as the ensemble. If I was to leave and another actor was to come in here and do another show, the ensemble would evolve in a weird shape to accommodate the change.

SAM: On the same lines, I'm enjoying doing this show so much, but it doesn't necessarily for me personally reflect my particular artistic choice. It's the not the way I would choose to present something, but the director had a very clear way of how he wanted the pace of the show, the volume of the show, the speed, and so forth, and so I feel like I wrote, or tried at least, to tailor what I like to do in that vein. I was curious about that too. What is our role as writers? Is this show reflective of the director's vision and we are tools that he uses? Or is he the one who organizes our artistic voice so that we have a wide palette of different colors?

JEAN: It's so fluid and that's what's really wonderful and really frustrating about working here.

ANDY COBB: I think there's also an element of, what is the cast willing to give? I think it sucks when directors have to come in and prove themselves. Like, fuck you. You're an actor. I'm the director. Why don't you suck my dick?

ANNE: This may be one of the only places where the actors have that much more power than the director does.

PETER: That's because we're writing though.

KLAUS: I find that any director who comes in here with a preset notion of what this show is going to be has set a horribly difficult task for themselves. They're going to try and take all these disparate energies and cram them into a little box and that's really hard.

KEEGAN: When the director sculpts what the actors have created. It's almost like Michelangelo having a supervisor standing over his shoulder who says, "I'll be back at four o'clock and I'll take a look at what you did." And then Michelangelo does all the work and there's sweat, blood, and tears, and then Luigi comes in and takes the chisel and the hammer and goes *pa-tink,* "All right, you're good. I'll see you tomorrow at four o'clock." And then he comes in tomorrow at four o'clock and then a lot more is done and he just does *pa-tink, pa-tink.* Yes, Luigi commissioned the sculpture so he's the director of the sculpture. But what if instead of *pa-tink, pa-tink* on the sculpture, what he actually does is walk through the room and say, "Ooh, Mike," and then moves a light toward the sculpture and he doesn't touch the work. The work stays intact, but he makes it clearer. He gives it a sense of clarity. "Let me move this light, open this shade, and when you have people come look at it, have them come in through that door and not this door."

NYIMA: I think a good director will also trick you into doing things you didn't know you could do. And you're like, at the end of the show, "Oh wow, I didn't even know I could do that" or "I didn't know I was that sort of person" or "I see in myself things that I saw in other people that I didn't know that I could do," roles that I didn't know I could play. And they kind of sneak it in on you.

SAM: That's kind of what Josh did with *Holy War, Batman!* because [Touring Company actor Kevin] McGeehan was assistant directing so he would hear Josh's ideas. Kevin and I would walk home from rehearsal together a lot and a lot of times, I would go, "Guess what we came up with today—we're gonna open with 'The Ocean.'" And he'd say, "Yeah, I knew about that in preproduction." I was like, "What? But we just came up with that idea today."

JEAN: That is the ideal thing for a director to do—to allow you to feel you've discovered something while they have control over it.

ANNE: I want to go back to the process. When you're coming in with an idea, how does that get translated into improvisation? Your first improvisation. How do you go from an idea to an improvisation?

ANDY: It's weird because I've had a number of different kinds of experiences where like, bring an idea in, partner not pleased with it, not improvising it well. You know, sometimes you have to drag it kicking and screaming into fruition. But ideally it seems like you can bring in a script to the process, you can bring an idea to the process, you can bring in like a suggestion of a way to improvise into the process, and they would all be capable of being turned into scenes. But that's ideal and doesn't happen often.

ANNE: What do you find most useful for yourself? Does it start with doing a scene in a montage and then you turn that into something; you do a pure improvisation that you turn into a scene? Do you come in with an idea?

PETER: I think it's good to have good premises. There's something about good premises; it's almost like they exist already. They get to the heart of the idea. The premise for Aerobics is incredibly simple. "We used to date and you're in my aerobics class and the things I do as the teacher all have to do with how pissed off I am at you."

KEEGAN: Sometimes what will happen is you will clutter the premise with a concept. Sometimes you have an activity, and two people who have an attitude about it or each other, and it starts to get toward a place that's known as premise-land. But sometimes we'll have an idea and a concept and an and, and an and, and an and. What seems to work for me is when the idea of the scene is intrinsic to the activity.

JEAN: What seems to be intrinsic to the premise to me is the game of the scene. If you don't have something you can heighten, [if you don't] have an idea, a joke, or an idea that's funny, it is not going to get you very far. Once you have the game of the scene, you can feed it and fuel it.

PETER: Good premises make you want to do a scene right away. You know, here's the premise. "Ooh, yeah, yeah, yeah."

KEEGAN: "Ooh, buddy, I got an idea! I got an idea!" That sense of delicious anxiety.

PETER: Yeah, it hits you in the brain.

KEEGAN: Or if someone gives you the premise and you say, "Oh my god, oh my god. Can I be a milkman?" And you don't even know what you're going to do. You just know that if you're a milkman you can feed it.

ANNE: What do you wish you had known, that somebody had told you before going into your first Second City process? I look back on the first Second City show I directed—all The Second City shows I directed— and I think, I was so stupid, I should have known....

NYIMA: I wish I had known that I could present a different opinion on-stage than what I feel. It's actually stronger to play the opposite. Say for example something happened to me on the street today and I bring that idea in—sometimes it's better for me to play the other person in the scene than to play myself because you find a lot more.

SAM: I wish someone had told me to bring things in. I think I came in with such a student mentality that the first process I waited for was an as-signment. And the second process was when I realized, no, I'm going to bring in absolutely every idea I have because six out of the nine are go-ing to get shot down but three will be okay . . . so just bring in anything.

ANDY: Come in and be a professional. Know what your job is and do your job. Remember that everything else is bullshit. And I was going to say, shots on goal. The more things you put up there . . . you know, there's a great line in *Heart of Darkness*—"History is not going to remember this work by what misses. It's going to remember what hits." So just keep try-ing to hit.

JEAN: It's so important to learn to fail and know how important failure is to get to the goal.

PETER: I think it's good to have a process that allows for change and failure and even, "Here's an idea. Here's a premise." "Oh, I have a similar prem-ise that is off that one and we'll just leave the first one in the dust be-cause it's not working." Allow the groove and flow. 'Cause that's what we have the ability to do and there's no reason to stifle that unique Second City aspect.

KEEGAN: I felt there was a formula for certain things and the only formula is "trust the ensemble." I wish I had known that for my first five shows. I would have more hair if I had been able to learn that.

Putting Up a Traditional Second City Improv Set

There are as many ways to put up a Second City improv set as there are companies of improvisers; what follows is a rough guideline of one ver-sion.

Take suggestions from the audience (generally four categories). These sug-gestions can be as banal as locations, occupations, and so on, or as interesting as "What do you fear most about the U.S. government?" Try looking for interesting ways to yield the following four general categories: environments, social or political topics, something stylistic, and something spiritual or meaningful to the audience (or something silly).

In the first five minutes of planning, brainstorm and riff off the suggestions. Don't push or pitch scene ideas. Just let the suggestions remind you of stories, things you've read, concerns you want to share. Use this time to get the cast thinking with a group mind.

Spend the next five minutes pitching scene ideas. The stage manager (or designated cast member) writes down a key word or phrase for each idea. Don't judge the ideas at this point; just get as many of them down as possible. "Yes, and . . ." everything. You can waste a lot of time here by saying no.

Pick from your list the scenes you want to use for your set and cast them. It is perfectly acceptable to pull blackouts from your cast "archives" to keep the set flowing. Remember to include one or two cast scenes per set. For show purposes, you may want to close with a high-energy improv game (Switch, Make a Musical). Assume that each scene or game will last approximately five minutes. For a twenty-minute set you should plan on four scenes plus blackouts and introductions.

Spend the next five minutes planning scenes. Plan the group scenes first and then split into smaller groups. Use your time economically; don't plan too much. Take a short moment to do any personal planning you might need.

The stage manager (or designated cast member) sets a running order. At this time, discuss with the stage manager (SM) and musical director any special cues or needs each scene might have. Give specific outs for blackouts and let the SM know if you want a scene to get to some event before he looks for the out.

You run the set. Remember, you are still improvising; if a scene goes off in an unexpected direction, follow it.

Using this process it should take you approximately twenty minutes to plan your set (about the length of time it takes for members of the show audience to leave, for the set audience to fill in empty seats, and for everyone to order a round of drinks). Keep track of the time; don't get bogged down in the brainstorming or pitching phases. Beware of overtalking ideas; let the scene develop onstage. Don't feel compelled to use all or even most of the suggestions. The idea is not to use as many suggestions as possible; the idea is to create compelling material. There is also a temptation to create high-concept premises by using two incongruous suggestions (see the Jim Game, on page 139). In general it is best to resist this temptation—these scenes are often more fun to anticipate than they are to actually improvise and often don't work unless the audience is clued in to the suggestions being used before the scene begins.

Blackouts and Extended Blackouts

A blackout is a short one-joke scene. The lights go out on the joke. A blackout should start with a seemingly obvious or cliché image or line of dialogue. Almost immediately thereafter something is done or said that either reframes the action or is blatantly inappropriate. For best results, the picture should be equally clear to the audience both before and after reframing.

Blackout Example 1: Reframing ("Kids")

MOM AND DAD: Bye! Bye! Take care! Call us!

DAD: I hate those people! They're rude. They have horrible manners. Did you smell that guy? He could knock a buzzard off an outhouse. And she . . . she had spinach between her teeth all night. Honey, you didn't serve spinach! I never want to see those people in this house again.

MOM: But, honey, they're our children.

Blackout Example 2: Inappropriate Response ("Morning Person")

[*Richard Kind enters singing and dancing to the tune of "Broadway Baby."*]

RICHARD: I'm a morning person! I wake up with the dew! I'm a morning person. I can't wait to see what's new! I say hello to . . .

[*Bonnie Hunt enters in a bathrobe and shoots him.*]

An *extended blackout* (EBO) is a blackout that requires a longer setup. Most of the time when we think we have an extended blackout, we have a blackout that needs editing.

A *runner* is a series of blackouts (usually three) interspersed throughout the running order.

How to Bottle Lightning for Fun and Profit

There's really little or no written information available to a young director or performer beginning his or her first show process. The veterans in the cast provide examples and you get some advice from others around the theater like Sheldon Patinkin or Bernie Sahlins. But mostly you end up making it up as you go along. I must confess that one of my hidden agendas in putting together this book was that it gave me a chance to find out how other Second City ensembles worked and to poke into a variety of different views and opinions about the process. Chris Earle is one of the most popular and accomplished directors for our theater in Toronto. My husband and I have had drinks with him and his wife, Shari Hollett, when they have been in Chicago for various reasons, but until now I never had the chance to get his very clear and cogent take on writing through improvisation.

Everything I needed to know about writing I learned at Second City. As a performer with the Toronto company in the early nineties, I discovered that improvisation could be more than just an end in itself; that it could also be a process whereby performers who'd never considered themselves writers could create funny satirical scenes complete with all the trappings of a written script—characters, dialogue, and structure—and that they could do this not by putting pen to paper but by playing in front of an audience. It seemed miraculous to me until I remembered that I'd done it before: when I was seven years old. Writing from improv was the way I'd spent a lot of my childhood: thinking up silly little scenarios and playing them out with my siblings in our parents' basement; classic scenes like Cops and Robbers, Zombies from Space, and of course House. We just never bothered to write the scripts down afterward. At Second City I rediscovered the process, and even got paid for it. And sometimes I even wrote down the scripts.

Improviser or Author?

In one sense, all writing is improv. Whether you're winging it onstage in front of a live audience or sitting alone in front of a laptop, the process of creating a story or scene using only your imagination is inherently improvisational. The writer/performer and the solitary author are both creating something from nothing—spontaneously making choices about character and action with no clear idea of where the story is going. Both are making it up. But there are a couple of big differences between them:

> The solitary author usually works alone. The improviser is always collaborating: with his scene partners, with his director, and with the audience.

> The author is not constrained by time. She can write as quickly or as slowly as she wants. She can even stop time, take a break in mid-sentence, and resume the next day—or the next year. Improvisers, meanwhile, are always prisoners of time, specifically, theatrical time. In front of an audience or in front of a director in rehearsal, the improviser is working against the clock. Once they begin a scene, they must adhere to theatrical time until the lights go out or the director lets them off the hook by calling out "Scene." They have no opportunity to pause and reflect on a choice, or to savor a particularly witty joke. Their awareness of themselves as writers is utterly subordinate to their job as performers. As performers there is no rest until the story has been told—until the scene, whatever its outcome, is over.

> The author usually creates characters for others to perform, while the improviser is always writing for himself. With improv, the script and the performance are largely inseparable, and it is of no concern to the improviser whether another performer can bring his character to life. In fact, all the better if he's the only one who can play the part—the more insurance against being replaced.

Both the solo author and the writer/improviser can create great work, but as someone who's used both methods I can tell you one thing: writer/improvisers have more fun.

Starting Out: Houston, We Have a Premise

The question students and actors ask most often in creating material is, "Do we have enough of a premise to make this scene work?" While it's impossible to predict what premises will turn into great scenes, here are a few thoughts:

Improvising with the goal of creating a finished scene or script requires the same ingredients as pure open improv: namely a Who, What, Where all linked together by a scenic premise. But the writer/improviser has to be even more exacting when it comes to premise because her quest is to create a scene that works not just once, *but night after night after night.* Open improv has a wonderful energy and life all its own; it's an art form where the medium truly is the message. When the audience watches improv their delight derives as much from their awareness that the performers are making it all up on the spot as from the scene itself. The electricity between the audience and performers depends on that awareness, and that sense of risk is what makes great improv so exciting. But when you're improvising as a means to write, this excitement can be a red herring, and the inexperienced performer can have trouble distinguishing between a laugh that comes from premise and thus advances the scene and an "improv laugh," where the audience laughs at what the performer is trying to accomplish, instead of something the character has done. An open improv can sometimes succeed without a complete premise; the finished scene will not.

Don't wait for the perfect premise. All too often, performers torture themselves by striving to think up the perfect premise: the brilliant, original idea that, once you think of it, just pretty well writes itself. This is a hopeless quest. The perfect premise does not exist. There are, however, a lot of very good premises (usually very *simple* premises) that with the right combination of character and relationship and environment will turn into a wonderful scene. Most great scenes emerge from simple, fairly ordinary premises. Find one and go for it.

The premise you begin with is seldom the one you end up with. Most of the good scenes I've helped create began with a very different premise. Almost all scenes either find or refine their premise during the improvisational process, and often the fact that a premise isn't evolving from draft to draft is a warning sign that it's not growing the way it should. An example: when I was putting up my first Mainstage show in Toronto, Nick Johne and I were working on a two-hander that we thought was very promising. I played an engineer for a huge utility company who encounters a Native American (played by Nick) while lost in the woods in northern Quebec. The humor came out of the culture clash between Nick's politically savvy Native American and my naive city slicker, and while it was funny enough to us, after a few times in front of an audience the scene was already getting stale. Nick and I kept trying to think up funnier jokes or make clever topical references, but it wasn't helping. The fact was, we didn't really have a complete premise. Sure we had a Who, and a Where, but we didn't have a What: What was the problem faced by the characters? What was the mutual activity that would connect them? What did they want from each other? The answers were "Don't know," "Not sure," and "Not much." And because we were unwilling to change the premise to create a stronger What, the scene died.

A happier example comes from directing a recent Mainstage show in Toronto. Cast members Paul Constable and Aurora Browne were working on a scene about a boring husband so complacent in his marriage that he could do his taxes at the kitchen table while his wife—in a vain attempt to attract his attention—did the dishes in the nude. It was funny, but pretty well-trod territory and the scene didn't seem to have much of a future. Then one day they decided to up the ante with a far stronger premise: in a bid to revive their sex life, the husband and wife resort to faking near-death experiences to arouse their passion. Same characters, same problem, but a much more interesting activity. Because of Paul and Aurora's willingness to ditch the old premise (and all the old jokes), a much better scene was born.

This story also illustrates one of the most important lessons of the improv/writing process. Learn to *let things go*. Much of your success as a writer/performer will depend on your ability to be a ruthless editor: to cut the hilarious joke that doesn't forward the scene; to overhaul the clever premise that isn't working; to cut the scene that's really just an excuse to trot out your favorite character. The ability to constantly try out and discard ideas is one of the great advantages to the improv process. Don't cheat yourself by clinging to material or ideas that are second best. There are always other jokes and other premises just around the corner.

Can I Start without a Premise?

Absolutely. If you've got great characters but no premise, don't just sit around trying to think up one. Make sure your characters have a strong point of view, give them a simple mutual activity, and set them loose. A lot of premises are discovered only after a scene has been improvised several times. Eventually something will suggest itself, and you'll find that clever twist that takes the scene to a whole new level.

Conversely, your premise might be strong, but the characters you've chosen to play it might be the problem. In Toronto, Carolyn Taylor and Jennifer Goodhue were struggling with a scene called Know-Nothings, in which they played a couple of ignoramuses in a Laundromat trying to talk about global politics. The scene was fun, but the women were such blissful idiots that there was little or no tension in the scene, because there was nothing at stake. Finally, just a few days before opening, we adjusted the premise so that they were no more ignorant than the majority of our audience. That is, they knew vaguely of certain issues and news stories, but their grasp of them was tenuous at best. Then we put David Shore in the scene, switched the location to a party, and endowed the characters with a desperate desire to *not look stupid. Et voilà*—suddenly the characters had something to lose (their self-esteem), and the audience recognized themselves in a way they hadn't before. Making those characters more believable and vulnerable made the scene work.

The Second City Process

While you may not have the opportunity to create material as a member of a Second City company, it's worth talking about the improv/writing process we use as a template for your own rehearsals. Essentially, the process can be divided into five parts:

EXPLORATION

The first few times a scene is taken out in front of an audience (or in rehearsal with a director), the actors are exploring character and premise. At this point, the improvisations should be as open and unstructured as possible. As I mentioned earlier, you may still be searching for the premise: trying out different locations, activities, relationships, and characters. These improvs are about discovering which choices add to the scenic point of view, raise the stakes for the characters, and focus the sharpness of the satire or comment. When in doubt, ask yourself this question: "What is this scene about?" The closer you get to the answer, the closer you'll be to the scene.

IMPROVISING THE PREMISE

You've done the exploration. You've got characters and a premise that reveal point of view. You know what the scene's "about." Now you can focus on heightening the premise as much as possible. You can start to make choices about the plot of the scene: how exposition is revealed, what tactics your characters use to fight for their objectives, and where the climax comes. If your premise is sound, you should be able to improvise afresh each time and find new beats and jokes. This is the part of the process where you should be generating more stuff than you'll need. The more you discover, the more options you'll have when it comes time to beat out the scene.

BEATING IT OUT

It's structure time. Grab a pen and paper, sit down with your scene partners, and figure out what happens in the scene from beat to beat. Try and keep it very simple—a list of what the characters *do* in the scene from moment to moment. Resist the urge to write down dialogue. Don't lock that in until the last possible moment. Improvising from beats is tricky—since from here on in you'll be doing less and less improvising and more and more acting. Try and keep to the beats, but stay loose and in the moment—and if you get the impulse to jettison a beat and go for something better, do it.

Scenically, this is where the men are separated from the boys. Do the beats work every time? Are they actable? Or are they improv moments that fade in the stretch? The audience (or your director) will let you know.

REFINING

Now you can really focus on the nitty-gritty. You and your scene partners know the beats. Now you can refine every moment. You might want to actually script the scene at this point—or you might not need to; my favorite process is where you've gradually scripted the scenes in your head through repeated improvising. No need for a script because everybody knows how it goes. Beautiful.

I should mention at this point that the process is seldom as straightforward as I describe here. There are times when you think you're at the refining stage when you suddenly realize you've got to go back and rethink the whole premise. There are even instances (too few in my career) where scenes seem to emerge fully formed after a couple of improvs. If a scene comes that easily, don't worry about it. Just thank the comedy gods and start working on something else.

PERFORMANCE

The best thing about scenes created through improvisation is how much they can evolve and grow through performance. As a performer at Second City I was always struck by how, in the course of a long run, the scenes that stayed fresh and fun to play were usually the ones created through organic improv. There was something about the way the material was developed, with a basis in truth and character that kept these scenes alive even after months of performance. Conversely, it seemed that the more a scene was scripted using conventional writing, the quicker it would grow stale. I think a lot of this has to do with the amount of subconscious texture that goes into an improvised scene. Things happen in improvs that nobody would ever think up sitting in front of a computer screen: subtleties of physicality and gesture and intonation that surprise and delight the audience. Details that only the performer, working *inside* character, can discover. It's why I think The Second City is truly an actor's theater, as opposed to a playwright's or a director's theater. The actor and what he or she can create through improvisation is always the center of the work.

—*Chris Earle*

AN IMPROVISATIONAL ALMANAC: PART SIX

For object transformations, use what shouldn't be there.

❧ ❧ ❧

You can prove anything in terms of anything.

❧ ❧ ❧

The more you tell an audience, the less they can imagine it. So we are searching for that privileged spot of Muhammad's coffin between heaven and earth.

❧ ❧ ❧

If you follow a fantasy long enough it becomes real.

❧ ❧ ❧

Be careful not to win the game at the cost of going off the board.

❧ ❧ ❧

Through theater, mirrors become prisms.

❧ ❧ ❧

If you are completely lost onstage, then obviously you should be. Do a scene on being lost. Realize that the next best thing to perfection is being damn good at what you do.

❧ ❧ ❧

All masks are empty until they are put on and inhabited by the actor.

❧ ❧ ❧

If you are always turning something into something you can never see what it is becoming. All your characters in your dreams understand your dream better than you do.

❧ ❧ ❧

There is no idea as good as the inevitable. So, if in the middle of someone else's beat you have the great idea, let it sit a while. It may fit or it may not. If it is the right idea and it is the correct one, then it will be able to fit in. If it was incorrect or untimely, waiting will prove that it may just have been a comment on the action.

   ❧ ❧ ❧

Try to remember to incorporate rhythm, at any and all levels. Each character, moment, entrance, exit, and line has an internal momentum and rhythm.

   ❧ ❧ ❧

One aim of religion is the method of science and the medium of theater. One original function of theater was to find and focus on the problems and information of being human in the current state. The truth of improvisation is about people. The objects, forms, structures, environments, games, characters, and processes all lead us to these various truths.

   ❧ ❧ ❧

A dream found is a dream lost.

CHAPTER SEVEN: **DIRECTING**

Most people think of directing as a control function. Really, at Second City, it's more of a facilitative function (at the risk of making up a word)—being a facilitator and helping people recognize their best work as opposed to telling them how to do it or how you see the show. Traditionally, we think the director takes a piece of material, interprets it, and then finds actors to fulfill his or her vision of it. That's not Second City. You have people who are constantly firing new ideas out. You help them catch the best ones and shape them and maybe see connections that they don't see and then give it a kind of polish. That's my experience.

—*Harold Ramis*

This is the worst, most inefficient way to create a show . . . ever.
    —*Jeff Richmond, during rehearsals for a Mainstage revue he was directing*

Directing for The Second City is quite possibly one of the most difficult direct-ing jobs that exist. The ideal Second City director is supposed to make bril-liant creative choices and then find a way to convince the performers that it was all their idea. Still, there is a fascination to the job that draws you back even when you've sworn "never again"—the excitement of watching material created by a group of brilliant improvisers in rehearsal and onstage each night in the improv sets; the puzzle of figuring out how to shape an improvi-sation into a scene and the even more complicated puzzle of creating a run-

During [the process of directing] *The Psychopath Not Taken,* I was beginning the second act for about three weeks with a fifteen-minute, two-person scene —improvised. We worked on these scenes and gave them the credence they deserved. It's the way you contextualize it. If you invite the audience to go on the ride with you and say, "This is the kind of thing now, will you join us?" they will.

I believe that we underestimate our audiences sometimes. We have certain constructs for them that just aren't true because we haven't provided a party for them to come to. We haven't provided a place for them to feel safe and a road map to follow in order to feel okay going on that journey with us.

—*Mick Napier*

ning order that supports and sets up a context for each individual scene. Oh, and it's supposed to be hysterically funny while you're at it.

I have a theory that the best Second City directors are the left brains in a sea of creative right-brained performers. Most of the successful directors here have been mathematically minded, enjoying logic puzzles, crossword puzzles —Mick Napier is fascinated by physics and computer programming. Jeff Richmond and Josh Funk are musicians. Ron West was often jokingly known as Dr. West or the Doctor long before he played a doctor on television's Third Rock from the Sun. *The shows that Ron has directed for The Second City are known for being smart, tightly constructed, and inventive in their use of the physical conventions of revue comedy. Some of the most popular scenes used by our touring companies are from shows that Ron directed. More than any other director I can think of, Ron West knows how to structure individual scenes so that they work perfectly every time they're performed.*

Blessed Obstacles

SCENE ONE

[*Lights up.* PHIL *sits in* RON's *office.*]

PHIL: I just got hired to direct a show at The Second City.

RON: I'm sorry.

PHIL: I'm not. It's going to be a lot of fun.

RON: I hope you have a lot of obstacles.

PHIL: You're trying to jinx me.

RON: Hardly. If you encounter obstacles, you are solving the problems in the script of your show. What you perform for the audience is a presentation of your solutions. There are a lot of obstacles along the way but happily there are ways to overcome them. The first obstacle to Putting On Your Comedy Show is the biggest obstacle.

PHIL: Tell me what it is.

RON: It's impossible.

PHIL: Oh, come on.

RON: Luckily, most of the people you're working with don't know it's impossible.

PHIL: That's good.

RON: But you don't have a script and you have limited time to write and rehearse. And a number of people in the cast have never written before.
And you have a tremendous legacy to live up to.

PHIL: That sounds impossible.

RON: So I have convinced you.

PHIL: We'll improvise the whole show. The audience loves that.

RON: You've never done this before, have you?

PHIL: Well, in college . . .

RON: Look, tell me the goddamn truth.

PHIL: No, I haven't done this before.

RON: Does the producer know that?

PHIL: No.

RON: You already have mastered the first lesson.

PHIL: Lie to the producer?

RON: No, but that doesn't hurt. The first lesson is always say, "Yes, I know
how to do that," even if you don't know how to do it.

PHIL: Okay, I know how to direct.

RON: I know you're lying, but go on.

PHIL: How do I generate the material? I only have twelve weeks.

RON: I like an eight-week rehearsal process.

PHIL: Why?

RON: Because everyone gets tired and reaches a point of diminishing re-
turns. Because the deadline forces you to get it done. And I don't want to
spend any more time in that freezing theater than I have to.

PHIL: But how do I generate the material?

RON: What, you don't have a script?

PHIL: No.

RON: Oh, that's right, someone tricked you into directing at Second City.

[PHIL *says nothing but looks very scared.*]

RON: One thing I like to do is review the scenes the cast has already improvised long before I've arrived on the scene. I spend the first week or two
of rehearsal looking at what amounts to rough drafts. Then I'll work on
the ones that interest me or that lead us to other ideas. Between these
presentations, what we brainstorm, and what we hit on in the set, I like
it when I am dealing with about a hundred pieces of raw material. The

final show usually has about twenty-two units. See? I've reduced to simple mathematics. Off you go now, and write your show. Time's a'wastin'!

PHIL: Why are you pressuring me?

RON: This is not pressure. Pressure is when St. Peter says to you, "What did you do to deserve a place in heaven?" This is fun. See what fun it is?

PHIL: Okay, do you just pick out the scenes you like, then?

RON: I think it would be more accurate to say I pick out the scenes I want to rewrite. I try to make the raw scene richer. I try to make the raw scene simpler. Sometimes simplifying it makes it richer. Sometimes I'll say, "Don't short-sheet that idea," which means I feel I'm not getting everything I want out of the sketch. But if a scene tries to accomplish too much, I'll say "That's too many taste treats in one," which is a line from a commercial for gum or mints.

PHIL: Really?

RON: Yes, really.

PHIL: I thought you just transcribed the scenes from the improvised set and put them in the show.

RON: That is a myth whose promulgation I won't abet. Some blackouts and some shorter scenes don't need rehearsal, I guess, but all the scene-length things need rehearsal and rewriting. The only scene I did that we never rehearsed was a cast scene called "Iron John." We just looked at the tape and put it in the show. It was a good scene created with ease by a mature ensemble.

PHIL [*dazed*]: I thought you just transcribed the scenes from the improvised set and put them in the show.

RON: Sorry.

PHIL: So how do you rewrite the scenes and make them richer?

RON: Once the cast presented a scene/song where two sewer workers, underground and unseen by the audience, interrupted their work to sing about their shared interest in Disney movies. So the joke was two macho guys singing about love for silly kids' movies. The song was fun, but the sewer workers were "made up" or "manufactured" and I still don't know why they were unseen by the audience. I changed the sewer workers to Arafat and Netanyahu and put Madeleine Albright in the room with them. Now the song was about two sworn enemies who stumble on a catalyst for peace. I guess this is an example of raising the stakes (peace in the Middle East is at stake in the scene). So you might give the scene a different context, show a clear grappling hook to reality (I love saying that), and make a complex subject very simple. In the case of Disney, the audience appreciated satiric solution to a world problem.

PHIL: So it became richer and simpler at the same time.

RON: Yes.

PHIL: And it's musical.

RON: Yes, and let me caution you there. The cast will want to do a lot of musical numbers. A musical number decorates the show, as Barb Wallace said. It is not the spine. Try not to spend too much precious rehearsal time on musical numbers.

PHIL: And music is only one of the things that makes Disney work.

RON: Right. In its earliest state, it was kind of funny that two unseen construction workers would sing about their love for Disney movies. In the rewritten version, it was *very* funny that the bitterest of enemies would stumble on a catalyst for peace. In general, shoot for *very funny* instead of *kind of funny*.

PHIL: How do you know the difference?

RON: Look at this chart. I've worked out all the variables mathematically.

PHIL: You have?

RON: You're very gullible.

[*Blackout.*]

SCENE TWO

[*Lights up.* PHIL *sits in* RON's *office.*]

PHIL: This is impossible.

RON: Yes, I remember telling you that.

PHIL: I don't know what to do.

RON: Oh, all of a sudden I'm your best friend.

PHIL: Please, don't ridicule me, I'm very fragile. The cast has created a scene called "Dirty Sanchez" that they love, but I hate it.

RON: That's good for two reasons. One, despite your hatred the scene won't die, so it might be valuable to the show. Two, it's a cast scene, and you need cast scenes.

PHIL: I have three.

RON: You need more.

PHIL: I do?

RON: Do I have to get out the scientific chart?

PHIL: Why do I need cast scenes?

RON: Because there's power in the group scene. Because there's six people you need to keep reintroducing to the audience. Because you're paying them to be onstage, not sitting around backstage watching TV. Because the audience loves seeing the group work together like a basketball team. Sure, one guy might score, but it is a group effort. Because your best resource/production value is the actors. Because it's more like theater and less like TV when they work together onstage. Because as a director there are a lot more options open to you with a group scene.

PHIL: Okay, well in this group scene called "Dirty Sanchez"...

[PHIL *describes the scene and re-creates most of the dialogue.*]

PHIL: ...and we don't have a blow.

RON: Okay, to save you a lot of embarrassment, I'll leave the details of the scene out of the essay.

PHIL: Thanks.

RON: It seems to me you might make your life easier if you decide what the scene is about.

PHIL: It's about being funnier.

[RON *hits* PHIL.]

RON: Never say that again. Your scene might be about something very sad or very serious that you will explore in a comedic way. We did a scene once that we called "Von Trapp"—in the opening night running order it was called "The Strange Case of Doctor Simon Barris." There were a lot of geeky characters and the cast loved it, but we couldn't finish it until we concluded that it was merely a scene about good triumphing over evil, which led us to two new beats and impacted the beginning and the closing.

PHIL: We've got a good beginning to "Dirty Sanchez."

RON: No, you don't. What you've done is lay a lot of pipe, but it doesn't go anywhere. Either use it or lose it.

PHIL: By "you" you mean me and the cast.

RON: If that makes you feel better, sure. In "Von Trapp," the geeky characters had powers and it was in rehearsal where we decided what those powers were, how they would be demonstrated, and what their impact was on the middle and end of the scene.

PHIL: But the beginning of "Dirty Sanchez" gets laughs.

RON: Yes, but you don't have a middle, and you've admitted you don't have a blow. Having a beginning, middle, and end is important, and the place we usually fall short is the middle.

PHIL: By "we" you mean me.

RON: By "we" I mean The Second City, Phil.

PHIL: Can't you just answer things "yes" or "no"?

RON: Yes.

[*An uncomfortable pause.*]

PHIL: Okay, where I think I am falling short is the blow.

RON: First of all, I think that having an ending that destroys the audience is overpursued. In other words, I think you ought to be able to have a great Christmas even if your parents don't give you a car. In fact, not worrying about pursuing the blow led The Second City to some of the long-form elements that are currently in vogue in shows.

PHIL: So in other words, quitting made them winners?

[RON *hits* PHIL.]

RON: I think it would be more accurate to say they found another way to overcome an obstacle. Second, I don't believe that the "full circle" ending works all the time, but I do think that things you have set up earlier in the scene will contribute to the blow. In "Von Trapp," everyone remembers that we did the whole scene backward.

PHIL: You mean theatrically rewound it.

RON: Yes, but it wasn't an arbitrary stunt—though to be fair, it was a flippant suggestion of Ian Gomez's. The theatrical rewind came out of geeky kids using their powers to defeat evil.

PHIL: So the scene came a long way from its original form.

RON: Yes, to where the physicality of the scene and what it was about were indivisible. Hey, I've got good news for you.

PHIL: I need some.

RON: I hated "Von Trapp" when I first saw it.

PHIL: That is good news.

[*Blackout.*]

SCENE THREE

[*Lights up.* PHIL *sits in* RON's *office.*]

PHIL: So I cut "Dirty Sanchez."

RON: That's good.

PHIL: It is?

RON: Yeah. Now it will lead you to something else. One of my problems is I don't want to cut scenes I've grown attached to. Ask people I've worked with about "Oratorio" and "Shackleton." I kept waiting for them to succeed, like a hopeful parent who bought a lot of sports equipment for his untalented child. So you are less attached to scenes.

PHIL: Thanks.

RON: Don't get a big head.

PHIL: I won't because I don't have enough cast scenes.

RON: You never do. The day after the show opens you'll wish you had one more.

PHIL: What do I do?

RON: Try to cultivate as many group scenes as you can. This does *not* mean everyone stands onstage in a semicircle and has the same amount of lines, though that happens a *lot* during improvisations.

PHIL: It sure does.

RON: And that's okay, but when you are molding the transcription into a written scene, remember that there are major characters, supporting characters, and minor characters. In "Les Audience" from *Jean Paul Sartre and Ringo,* the major characters are Dexter and his dad. The supporting characters are Deirdre, Mom, and the art buyer. The minor character is Julian.

PHIL: I don't know that scene.

[RON *hits* PHIL.]

PHIL: I'm going to find that scene and read it . . .

RON: Good idea . . .

PHIL: . . . because right now in my cast scenes all the characters stand in a semicircle and have the same amount of lines.

RON: So you have been working all this time and your cast scenes are all the same.

PHIL: You sure paint a rosy picture.

RON: Don't worry. It happens all the time. It is common to find yourself with two or three or even four scenes that are essentially the same.

[PHIL *makes a silent horrible realization.*]

RON: What's wrong?

PHIL: Can we get back to "developing cast scenes"?

RON: Sometimes the running order can accommodate—a.k.a. hide—the fact that scenes are the same.

PHIL: Can we get back to "developing cast scenes"?

RON: Are you going to delay your opening?

PHIL: Can we get back to "developing cast scenes"?

RON: Sure. I suggest you do a day or two where you improvise cast scenes cold. Don't analyze them until you've done ten or even twenty. The only rule for these improvisations is that each actor must appear in each scene at some point.

PHIL: So it counts as a cast scene if they just enter as bystanders?

RON: I like the way you cheat. Another way to develop group scenes is a game called Seven-Up—because there were seven people in the room when we devised it. Do a scene based on any old suggestion. The scene will be over shortly after the last actor enters.

PHIL: Would that work as a performance game?

RON: Yes, but I don't think you should look at it as a panacea. When you start to analyze the scenes you've improvised, look at the pattern or the potential structure. By that I mean things like . . .

One character stays onstage the entire time. Sometimes I call him a control figure or facilitator. Each character that enters has a separate interaction with the control figure. So it is like a series of two- or three-person scenes. "Audition" from *Winner Takes Oil* is a good example.

Everyone is onstage the entire time. The facilitator acts like the host of a talk show. It is best when it seems like the host is struggling to keep up with a crazy dog on a leash. "Orchestra" from *Economy of Errors* is an example.

Each character has a separate entrance and stays on until the end of the scene. "Funeral" is an example.

There is a five-on-one dynamic where one person is ganged up on. "Polish" from *The Psychopath Not Taken* is a good example.

There is a one-on-five dynamic, where one person has authority over the others. "Afrikaans and Andy" from *Mayor-Go-Round* is an example.

One character goes on a journey to a number of locations.

PHIL: Like a *Wizard of Oz* parody!

[RON *hits* PHIL.]

RON: I am drafting legislature right now that would eliminate *Wizard of Oz* parodies from the comedy nomenclature.

PHIL: But in our show George W. is the Wizard and . . .

RON: Shut up or I'll kill you.

[*Pause.*]

RON: Where was I?

PHIL: Seven.

RON: Thank you.

One or more characters daydreams and everybody plays someone else in the daydreams. Be careful here: I don't like to see "scene within a scene" because it is hard enough to do one scene, let alone two. Also, I don't want anyone saying, "It was all a dream."

PHIL: Like they do in *The Wi* . . . go on, please.

RON: Thanks . . .

The organization of people in the scenic reality is something that everyone is basically familiar with and that controls the chaos, such as the drill sergeant reviewing troops or a courtroom situation.

Decide who the main character is and what he wants. The rest can enter and exit at will to help him get what he wants. Their efforts may or may not help the main character. The "what's beyond" will significantly effect what is happening onstage. See "Backstage" from *Exit, Pursued by a Bear.*

Does the scene have more than six characters? You can make a virtue out of having the actors play more than one character each. See "Pledge" from *Curious George Goes to War.*

This is by no means a complete list. But by "boxing" the pattern, you can exploit it and, ultimately, think outside the box. Once you know the pattern, you can layer the scene in its next incarnation.

PHIL: You mean, set the pattern before you change it. Know the rules before you break them.

RON: Yes, that's the idea. Try combining the models too. Once, John Hildreth wanted to do a scene where Jimmy Doyle instructed the audience in aerobics.

PHIL: That is number five on your list.

RON: Yes. In addition, we had asked the audience to play a specific character. To that I added the layer of a business meeting and a disgruntled employee who holds his boss hostage. To that, Scott Adsit and Ian Gomez played people who try to help the main character.

PHIL: That is number nine.

RON: Yes. Ian showed Jimmy how to use the gun ("like it's an extension of your arm," he said) and we had a good scene called "Workout" to close the act.

PHIL: Now I definitely have to delay opening because you just described *my* first-act closer. Has everything been done?

RON: Yes, I saw a scene very similar to "Polish" that was done fifteen years before "Polish." But it also took place over the course of time and locations.

PHIL: It seems like everything has been done.

RON: It has. But you can overcome that obstacle too.

PHIL: You are such a bastard.

RON: I am a really nice guy. Ask any of the girls who broke up with me.

[*Blackout.*]

—*Ron West*

Running Orders

When Bernie took over as a director, his statement was: "Put your best stuff up front but save something for the ends of the acts, please." Put [the smartest and the most politically relevant] stuff up front to establish the credentials of the show rather than the actors. Whereas Paul Sills's [state-

Getting the audience to like the cast early is just crucial so they can trust them to go on. I was reading *Nine Stories* and J. D. Salinger was talking about how he crafted the order for the stories in the book. As I was listening to what he was talking about, I was picturing myself backstage getting ready for a show and juggling cards. He was asking the same questions! Do you need this character to be liked here so you can laugh at him here? It was the exact same thing.

—*Tom Gianas*

ment] was: "Let's establish who the performers are and then surprise them with what else they can do."

—*Sheldon Patinkin*

Running orders are, quite simply, the order of the scenes within a given show. A good running order doesn't show itself as "good"—the show itself feels good, individual scenes show up at their best, and the evening has a sort of inevitable flow and arc to it. A bad running order can trash perfectly good material. What follows is a list of my own thoughts and opinions on building a running order—in no particular order.

- Your opening scene/game/musical number should be high energy, feature the full cast, and introduce the cast playing characters who are close to themselves.

- The audience should get a chance to see the entire cast at least twice within the first three scenes of the show.

- The last person to speak in a scene should not be the first person to speak in the following scene (the audience often assumes that they are the same character).

- Quick-and-dirty running order: alternate full-cast, high-energy scenes or games with smaller, less intense scenes or games.

- The more you get your entire cast onstage working together, the more the audience gets to know them and the more you can get away with. Put lots of full-cast stuff in the first act and you can take a lot more risks in the second act.

- No one act of an improv or sketch show should be more than fifty minutes long.

- Allowing five minutes per scene or game (plus room for a couple of freebie blackouts) is a good starting rule of thumb for rough-timing out an act or show. As you get to know your own group's timing better, you can adjust up or down from there.

- Your first few scenes teach the audience how to watch you.

- The most protected spot in the running order is the second scene of the second act. This is where Barbara Harris and Severn Darden used to have their relationship scenes in the original Second City shows. Don't put your weakest scene here; put your most delicate or meaty scene here. Any scene goes well in this slot.

- Your first-act closer doesn't have to be your funniest scene but it should send the audience out into the lobby talking.

- Your funniest scene is the last scene before your second-act closer (or the last scene before the closer if you are doing a one-act show).

- Runners need to work on their own and get progressively funnier. Otherwise, you don't have a runner, just various versions of the same joke.

- Monologues and solo songs are great—they stop the show both literally and figuratively. Too many and the rhythm of the show will feel jerky and awkward.

- A good blackout will give the show a burst of energy and help the audience sit through something longer and more serious.

- Callbacks are best when they do more than simply repeat something mentioned earlier in the show. Ideally, they present an old situation, character, or phrase in a new context.

- Fancy transitions, themes, recurring characters, and the like are terrific but you can't do them by halves. They should flow through the entire show or not at all.

- It's all about context.

- Your closer shouldn't be your funniest or best scene but it should get the entire cast back onstage and provide a natural end for the evening.

- Sometimes it just works and sometimes it just doesn't. You can follow all of these rules and still have a crappy running order and you can break them all and have one that works brilliantly. Sometimes you just have to fuck around, take a risk, and see what happens.

About ten years ago Tom Gianas directed the revolutionary production *Piñata Full of Bees* on the Chicago Mainstage and substantially changed the way that directors at Second City approach running orders. Not only was the content of *Piñata* a brilliant savage attack on a certain kind of American complacency, but individual scenes were split up into pieces and

I go crazy. At home, I pace for six hours and try to figure out how all these elements can come together, et cetera. You go on an hour jag and think you have energy of scenes, variety of characters, taking care of thematic contexts, connected up. Then at the end of an hour and a half or two hours you go, "Fuck! Kevin has his pants off! He can't get dressed for the next scene!"

—*Mick Napier*

woven throughout the show; characters and moments from early scenes were called back and connected into later pieces, with the whole culminating in a closer that connected the entire show literally and thematically.

Since then running orders have become even more difficult, as scenes are split into as many as six or seven parts; where once a running order consisted of seven or eight pieces an act, you could now have twenty-five pieces requiring precision in order to make logical sense as well as to build energy and momentum.

Ideal Running Order

The "ideal" running order that Norm Holly has put together works for both "old school" and "new school" shows—each slot can be filled by one scene or by a group of scenes that fulfill the same function. Norm is head of the Chicago Training Center Conservatory Program and my partner in crime in the light booth during student shows. He is a genius at helping actors take a pedestrian premise and find the hook that will make it hysterical (and often dark and twisted as well). I have heard Norm refer to certain particularly funny scenes as being the "Amnesia Slot"—you can put anything that isn't working just before that slot because the scene works so well that the audience forgets anything that came before.

Act One

Opening. The opening slot shows the performers as close to their own personas as possible. It also introduces, in a nonovert manner, the general theme of the show.

Bump. If the opening scene does not have a hard out, this slot should include one or more blackout-type scenes. This is also the intro slot, largely used to address the audience directly, welcoming them to the show. Very often this introduction displays an actor in his or her own persona when that actor is very character driven within the show.

Act One, Scene One. Introduces the audience of the revue to the skills the performers possess as actors as well as improvisers. This slot usually contains the lightest scene in the show, nonchallenging in content or execution.

Act One Skill Slot. Displays to the audience the ensemble's skills beyond revue scene form. Most often it will be a song or an improvised piece.

Speed Bump. Gives the first act forward movement. This tends to be a heavier laugh slot than any previously in the act. This also tends to be the slot in which the actors may first play more extreme characters, since they have at this point been set up as skilled actors and performers.

Act One, Scene Two. Revisits the style of the initial scene slot, but must extend it in content and execution. It may more obviously restate the theme of the revue.

Act One Run-Out. Speeds the first act into its conclusion. This slot echoes the skill slot, calling back the idea of very skilled performers while at the same time extending the speed and content of that earlier speed slot.

Act One Closer. Simply the funniest scene in the show. Not the best scene but the funniest. Though it is preferable to have this be a cast scene, that is not as important as that this scene be the most laugh heavy. The act one closing slot is the most important slot in the revue. It is what may or may not inspire the audience to return for the second act.

Act Two

Act Two Opener. The act two opening slot serves one purpose: to get the audience to look at the stage again. It is very often a loud blackout or extended blackout, or perhaps a throwaway song. Its only job is to get the audience's attention after intermission (or in one-act form, after what would be the act one closing scene). It is therefore important that the exposition at the top of the scene not be important to the execution.

Act Two, Scene Two. This slot extends the ideas and execution of the act one, scene one slot. It should be more challenging in content.

Act Two Skill Slot. This is a reminder to the audience that they are watching skilled performers, and again executes a skill that is perhaps unexpected. If it is again a song or improvisation, its degree of difficulty must surpass that seen in act one.

Stupid Slot. The slot in the show where anything goes. By this point the audience knows they are watching skilled dramatic and comic performers, and ideally they understand the theme of the show. What they are not expecting is for everything set up thus far to be thrown out the window. That can happen here.

Act Two, Scene Two. Simply the best piece in the revue. It culminates everything that has been set up thus far, and extends it contentwise in a way the audience is not expecting. It has been intentionally set up by the previous slot to be unexpected.

Act Two Run-Out. Must extend in form and content the act one run-out. There is little doubt to the audience that the revue is ending soon.

Act Two Closer. Completes the ideas of the revue. Often a "bookend" to the opener, it concludes the initial relationship and ideas set up early on. The act two closing slot must clearly end the show, leaving the audience feeling as if there is no more to do. It must not introduce new ideas; it must conclude unfinished business and give the sense that the show is over.

—Norm Holly

AN IMPROVISATIONAL ALMANAC: PART SEVEN

Characteristics help a character express basic emotional patterns.

Sharing the history of the character with the audience can be seen as spoon-feeding. Sharing the emotion with the audience brings the history out.

All acting is writing.

Actors must agree to the ironic point, agree to the opening, then go.

Every line should advance the scene forward.

The faster you greet the exposition and get it out of the way, the sooner the scene can start to fly.

When playing someone who is young, play as smart as an adult, and when playing an adult, try not to lose the childlike wonder at the world.

Let each moment or beat have its time in the space before allowing the next one to unfold.

Let every object have time, space, texture, and a life of its own. It is vital that you believe you are biting into a juicy peach and can feel the small bit running down your chin. This attention to detail is not exactly mime, but if you believe, the audience can't help but share in your belief.

There has got to be more, but I will let you make your own lists.

Peace.

ACKNOWLEDGMENTS

First and foremost, I wish to thank all the contributors who gave so generously of their time and talent. When the essays started arriving, there were days when opening my e-mail was like Christmas morning. Special thanks to the ETC cast for their time and their insight.

Two other people made very special contributions to this book: Shelley Schreiber, who allowed me full use of Avery's beginning and advanced syllabi (thanks to Karly Rothenberg for getting them here), and Patty de Maat, who gave me generous access to Marty's papers and words of encouragement at the onset of this project.

At The Second City Chicago:

Without Andrew Alexander and his continued support this book would not have been possible. Thanks to Robin Johnson for being the best producer anyone could have asked for on this project and to Beth Kligerman for her help with information and arrangements of all kinds. As always thanks goes to Joyce Sloane, for her memory, for her contacts, and for never throwing anything away. Thanks to Pat McKenna for the illustrations and to Dennis Javier for help with photos.

Thanks to Rob Chambers for his thoughtful notes, and to "The Guys" in the Training Center office—Ted Howard, Garrett Prejean, and Ranjit Souri—and the faculty of The Chicago Training Center, especially the "improv core"—Lillie Frances, Bob Kulhan, and Brian Posen.

Thanks to the members of The Second City touring companies who responded to my request for thoughts on games and long form, with a special shout out to Blueco.

At The Second City Toronto, Moira Dunphy, Steve Morel, Janice Rae, and Erin Lister were all a great resource for information and addresses.

At The Second City Los Angeles, Frances Callier helped me out early on and Lee Costello came in with a last-minute save.

Additional thanks goes to Ivan Dee, Jordan Jacobs, Susan Harris, Sue Betz, and Rachel Zonderman Delaney.

Personally, I need to thank Mary Scruggs and Sheila Flaherty for support and advice, both practical and inspirational; Colleen Grace for babysitting; and Matt Cullison for simultaneously babysitting and offering some very useful notes.

Thanks to my family—Julie Liss, David Libera, Joan Hershbell, Roy and Sheila Leonard, and my children Nicholas and Eleanor (who was born in the midst of this project and thus gave all the procrastinators a few more months to turn in their essays). I owe a special debt of gratitude to Kelly Leonard for the myriad of things he did to help in his dual capacities as producer of The Second City and as my husband, and for his ability to switch hats as the situation warranted.

Finally, I want to thank my students, who always teach me more than I could ever possibly teach them.

APPENDIX

Status Behaviors

What follows is a short list of status behaviors generated in improv classes. You can make your own. Once you get the hang of it, it's hard to stop.

High Status

Holds eye contact and when breaks eye contact doesn't look back

Holds head still

Holds head up/has good posture (looks down nose)

Turns back on someone he or she is talking to

Keeps chest and genital area open

Uses expansive gestures

Keeps shoulders back

Has little to no expression on face

Moves decisively (fast or slow but with a measured gait and sense of specific destination)

Keeps feet pointed slightly outward

Stands on two feet

When moving, cuts off person coming toward him or her

Is taller

Has a low voice (think Darth Vader)

Speaks in full sentences

Dominates conversation

Interrupts others

Accents: British (any), Boston, newscaster midwestern

Rolls eyes

Uses cell phone

Invades others' personal space

Points

Snaps

Enters a door before others

Downward gestures (pat on the head, pat on the shoulder, "getting the upper hand" in a handshake)

Most high-status word: "No"

Controls anger

Explains meaning

Low Status

Breaks eye contact

Moves head (nods)

Has slumped shoulders/bad posture

Protects chest/genital area

Smiles

Has facial tics

Blinks

Stands unevenly

Shifts weight

Crouches down (gets physically lower)

Is physically shorter

Actively works to not turn back

Bows

Meanders while walking

Takes tiny steps

Backs up

Gets out of the way

Fidgets

Grooms self

Bites fingernails

Chews lip

Touches face

Plays with hair

Burps

Hiccups

Drops things

Breaks things

Has a high voice

Has a voice that breaks

Uses "uptalk"

Interrupts self

Mumbles

Asks questions

Accents: Southern, black English, California surfer

Uses "um" and "uh" repeatedly

Finishes sentences with short questions (*Right?*)

Rambles vocally

Laughs

Cries

Is physically incapacitated in some way

Lets anger get out of control

Has a red face/blushes

Shows fear

Things We Do to Raise Someone Else's Status

Compliment them

Laugh at their jokes

Affirm them (say yes, nod)

Ask them questions

Things We Do to Lower Someone Else's Status

Insult them

Make fun of them

Hit them

Interrupt them

Criticize them

Correct them

RECOMMENDED READING

Coleman, Janet. *The Compass: The Improvisational Theatre That Revolutionized American Comedy.* Chicago: University of Chicago Press, 1991.

Halpern, Charna, Del Close, Kim Johnson, and Mike Myers. *Truth in Comedy: The Manual of Improvisation.* Colorado Springs, Colo.: Meriwether, 1994.

Johnstone, Keith. *Impro for Storytellers.* New York: Routledge, 1999.

Johnstone, Keith. *Impro: Improvisation and the Theatre.* New York: Theater Arts Books, 1989.

Kozlowski, Rob. *The Art of Chicago Improv: Short Cuts to Long-Form Improvisation.* Portsmouth, N.H.: Heinemann, 2002.

Napier, Mick. *Improvise: Scene from the Inside Out.* Portsmouth, N.H.: Heinemann, 2004.

Patinkin, Sheldon. *The Second City: Backstage at the World's Greatest Comedy Theater.* Naperville, Ill.: Sourcebooks Trade, 2000.

Sahlins, Bernard. *Days and Nights at The Second City.* Chicago: Ivan R. Dee, 2001.

Spolin, Viola. *Improvisation for the Theater: A Handbook of Teaching and Directing Techniques (Drama and Performance Studies).* Edited by Paul Sills. Evanston, Ill.: Northwestern University Press, 1999.

Sweet, Jeffrey. *Something Wonderful Right Away: An Oral History of The Second City and the Compass Players.* New York: Limelight Editions, 1987.

Vorhaus, John. *The Comic Toolbox: How to Be Funny Even If You're Not.* Los Angeles: Silman-James Press, 1994.

CONTRIBUTORS

ANDREW ALEXANDER recently served as an executive producer on the film *Whitecoats*. He took the reins of The Second City Toronto in 1974, and in 1976, he formed a partnership with Len Stuart, starting The Second City Entertainment Company. Its first television production was *SCTV*. Alexander codeveloped and executive produced more than 185 half-hour shows for the award-winning comedy series, and he produced more than 150 hours of award-winning television comedy. Alexander has coproduction deals with MGM Television, Imagine Films, Disney Studios, and United Artists, and he has developed television programming for ABC, CBS, NBC, FOX Television, Comedy Central, HBO, Showtime, A&E, and the Canadian Broadcasting Corporation. Alexander has produced movies and television shows with some of North America's biggest stars, including John Candy, Dan Aykroyd, Bonnie Hunt, Mike Myers, Chris Farley, Rick Moranis, Catherine O'Hara, Martin Short, Harold Ramis, Jim Belushi, George Wendt, Ed Asner, Andrea Martin, and Shelley Long. In 1985, Alexander became a co-owner of The Second City Chicago, expanding the theater division to include Cleveland, Detroit, Las Vegas, and Los Angeles. He has produced or executive produced more than 200 Second City revues in Canada and the United States. Most recently, Alexander has expanded The Second City television and film division with offices in Los Angeles and Toronto. He serves on the board of directors of Gilda's Club Chicago and is chair of the Gilda's Club Honorary Board in Toronto.

SANDRA BALCOVSKE started at The Second City as a writer/performer with the Edmonton company and the Toronto Mainstage. Sandra directed several touring companies, the London Company, the Expo '86 Company, and eight shows for the Toronto Mainstage. She has collaborated with other alumni on projects for stage and television. Sandra was creative advisor at The Second City Toronto for several years at the end of the last century.

DEXTER BULLARD teaches improvisation, acting, and physical theater at The Second City Training Center, DePaul Theatre School, and Plasticene, a critically acclaimed experimental physical theater company that he founded in 1995. Dexter has directed for The Second City ETC and The Second City Detroit, and spent three years with The Second City National Touring Company. Plasticene's improvisationally developed works have been featured at Steppenwolf Studio, Edinburgh Fringe Fest, and Storefront Theater, and in New York City.

Emmy Award–winner DAN CASTELLANETA is the voice of Homer Simpson . . . as well as Krusty the Clown, Grampa Simpson, Barney Gumble, Mayor Quimby, Groundskeeper Willie, and a multitude of others on the historic FOX series *The Simpsons*. A former cast member of *The Tracey Ullman Show* and *Sibs*, Castellaneta has also made numerous guest appearances on television shows including *Mad About You, L.A. Law, NYPD Blue, Wings, Murphy Brown, Friends, Cybill, The Drew Carey Show, ALF, Love & War, The George Carlin Show,* and *Married . . . with Children*. His television films include the Emmy Award–winning *Hand in the Glove*. His feature film work includes *My Giant, Space Jam, Forget Paris, The Client, The War of the Roses, K-9, Say Anything, Nothing in Common,* and Neil Simon's *Laughter on the 23rd Floor* for Showtime. Voice-over work includes the voices of Genie in the successful animated television series *Aladdin* and the sequel *The Return of Jafar*. Most recently, Castellaneta performed off-Broadway in *The Alchemist* with the Classic Stage Company. Early in his career he performed with the famous Chicago improvisation/comedy group The Second City. A native of Chicago, Castellaneta resides in Los Angeles.

ANDREW CURRIE joined the resident cast of The Second City Toronto in 1993 and wrote/performed in five revues. He received a Dora Mavor Moore Award nomination for outstanding performance for his work in 1995's *Jolly Rogers Cable*. Andrew and alum Albert Howell gained notoriety as The Devil's Advocates on Citytv's *Speaker's Corner*, then developed and hosted eighty episodes of Canada's first improv series for TV, *Improv Heaven & Hell*. Andrew continues working with Second City in teaching and performing; in 2001 he was invited to represent the Toronto company for its first-ever tour of Asia . . . and he's been invited back!

MARTIN DE MAAT began his study of improvisation at the age of nine in Chicago with Viola Spolin and began teaching at The Second City while still a teenager. He was a member of the creative staff at The Second City, holding positions as the artistic director of The Second City Training Centers and an artistic consultant to The Second City theaters. An accomplished director, freelance designer, design consultant, and facilitator, Martin held an artist-in-residency position at Columbia College Chicago and was a faculty member of New York's Video Associates and the Omega Institute. He was awarded an experiential Ph.D. in communication arts from the Advanced Studies Institute and the National University, Kanpur, India.

CHRIS EARLE is an alumnus of The Second City Toronto, where he currently teaches improv. He has also directed several Mainstage shows, including *Last Tango on Lombard* and *Psychedelicatessen*. Chris has worked extensively in the Toronto theater scene as an actor, director, and playwright.

TINA FEY was a member of The Second City Touring Company and The Second City Mainstage in Chicago, where she opened two revues, *Citizen Gates* and *Paradigm Lost*. She left Second City to become a writer on NBC's *Saturday Night Live,* where she was quickly named the first female head writer in the show's history. Tina also became cohost of the legendary "Weekend Update" segment of the show.

MICHAEL J. GELLMAN (Head of IFA, Special Workshops, and New York Programs) was a Resident Company member of The Second City Chicago for three years and he has directed at The Second City since 1980. He was nominated for Outstanding Director for the national Dora Mavor Moore Award in Canada and the Joseph Jefferson Award in Chicago, and he won the *Detroit Free Press* Award for Best Comedy. Michael served as artistic director of Chicago TheatreWorks and Wavelength and as an Artistic Associate of Organic Theater. In addition to The Second City Training Center, Michael has taught at Columbia College Chicago, Northern Illinois University, and Artistic New Directions.

A Second City alumnus, SHARI HOLLETT has been teaching improv at The Second City Toronto for more than ten years, is a former head of their Training Center, and has also directed the National Touring Company. She is an actor, a director, a playwright, and co–artistic director of The Night Kitchen Theatre Company.

NORM HOLLY (Co–Artistic Director, Head of Conservatory and Acting Programs) has directed Second City shows including *Baby Richards Got Back* and *40*

Oz. and a Mule. He was the assistant chairman of the Columbia College Chicago Theater Department for eight years and directed many productions there, including *Caucasian Chalk Circle* with Jeff Perry and Barbara Robertson and *Once in a Lifetime* with Michael Maggio. Norm appeared in the New Broadway Theater production of *Streamers* with Dennis Farina, directed by Terry Kinney. He was director of the live comedy series Anti-Comedy I/II/III with Dino Stamotopolous and Andy Dick, on-camera director for CineFolio (now Short), and director of Second City's NBC pilot as well as dozens of revue productions.

BRUCE HUNTER joined The Second City Toronto in 1981; in his twenty years as an instructor he has taught improvisation to thousands of students. He has taught at Humber College in the music and theater departments and has been a guest lecturer at the University of Toronto and Ryerson University. He has developed a series of classes in improvisation and text and he teaches in the industrial world for companies such as IBM, Eli Lilly, Bell Mobility, and Microsoft. Additionally, he produces, directs, acts, and writes throughout the United States and Canada. Bruce just finished playing the part of Mack, an FBI agent, in the upcoming William Hurt movie *Hanson.*

NICK JOHNE was a member of The Second City Toronto Mainstage cast from 1990 to 1993, performing and writing in four revues, two of which won the Dora Mavor Moore Award for writing and performance. He has studied clowning with Richard Pochinko and Sue Morrison, and has also studied le Jeu and Bouffon with Philippe Gaulier. He has been teaching at The Second City since 1993 and also currently teaches at the Humber School of Comedy.

Screenwriter/actor TIM KAZURINSKY got his start at Chicago's Second City Theater. Movie appearances include *Neighbors, About Last Night . . . , Somewhere in Time, Dinner at Eight, Shakes the Clown, Poor White Trash,* and three (yes, three) *Police Academy* films. He is also a former cast member and writer on NBC's *Saturday Night Live.* Tim's screenwriting credits include *About Last Night . . . , The Cherokee Kid,* and *For Keeps,* cowritten with Denise DeClue. Tim and his wife, Marcia, live in Evanston, Illinois, with a couple of cute kids, a dog, two cats, and a pet squirrel.

KEEGAN-MICHAEL KEY was a member of The Second City Detroit Mainstage for three years and eleven months, to the day, where he performed in and helped write eleven revues. He is now a member of The Second City ETC stage, where he has written two shows. He has also been an instructor at The Second City Detroit Training Center and is currently an instructor at The Second City Training Center in Chicago. Keegan-Michael also works with the Minority Outreach Program and Second City's corporate entity, Second City Communications, for which he also writes and performs.

FRANK McANULTY graduated from Seneca College with a degree in radio and television production. He worked as an assistant director on many television shows and as a cameraman for ABC's *Wide World of Sports*. In 1984 he decided to switch to acting and teaching and joined The Second City. Frank has been teaching improv and acting classes since 1985 at all levels from children's workshops to corporate workshops. He helped develop The Second City Workshop Centre in London, Ontario, which ran from 1985 through 1990. Frank also teaches corporate communication for many of Canada's largest corporations. He currently teaches improv and sketch comedy at Humber College.

ADAM McKAY moved to Chicago to study with Del Close at the ImprovOlympic Theater, where he was in the house improv group The Family for five years. He was a founding member of the Upright Citizens Brigade and a member of The Second City, where he was in *Piñata Full of Bees*. Adam was then head writer of *Saturday Night Live*, where he also directed a series of short films. He now lives in New York with his wife and daughter, writing screenplays and still occasionally sitting in on *Asssscat* at the UCB Theater on 22nd Street.

PATRICK McKENNA has worked at The Second City for just over ten years. He wouldn't trade a minute of it, especially the ones he spent with Lois. He is proud to be a part of this almanac.

SUSAN MESSING was a writer and ensemble member for two Second City Mainstage revues and has also directed for The Second City. She has performed with and created teaching curriculum for the ImprovOlympic and is a founding member of the infamous Annoyance Theater, originating roles in almost forty original productions. She has performed stand-up with her puppet Jolly at the HBO U.S. Comedy Arts Festival in Aspen and on Comedy Central and NBC. Her latest production is a baby.

MICK NAPIER is an award-winning director and renowned teacher, facilitator, author, and improviser. In addition to being the founder of Chicago's acclaimed Annoyance Theater and Annoyance Productions, Mick is also an artistic consultant for The Second City, where he has directed more than nine reviews including the fortieth-anniversary show *Second City 4.0.* For the 1996 production *Paradigm Lost,* he earned a prestigious Joseph Jefferson Award for his direction. Mick's experience in television and film include serving as writer/director for Cable Ace–nominated *Exit 57* for Comedy Central. He was the creative producer on the nationally syndicated sketch TV show *Sports Bar,* and he directed the live pilot for HBO/Comedy Central's *T.B.A.* Mick is author of the book *Improvise: Scene from the Inside Out.*

DAVID PASQUESI is an alumnus of The Second City, where he won a Joseph Jefferson Award for Best Actor in a Revue under the direction of Del Close. He has been improvising consistently since 1984, and continues to do so. His stage work includes *The Chicago Conspiracy Trial* at Remains Theater, *Glengarry Glen Ross* and *The Dazzle* at Steppenwolf, and *Great Men of Science* at Lookingglass. His own show, *Kill the Messenger,* after a Chicago run, went on to play the U.S. Comedy Arts Festival in Aspen. His television and film credits include *Father of the Bride, Groundhog Day, Strangers with Candy,* and *Employee of the Month.* He has improvised in three countries on two continents.

SHELDON PATINKIN currently serves as the Theater Department chair at Columbia College Chicago. He is also an artistic consultant to The Second City and Steppenwolf Theatre as well as part of the Acting Faculty at Lyric Opera Center for American Artists. Additionally, he has authored two books: *The Second City: Backstage at the World's Greatest Comedy Theater* and a forthcoming work on the history of American musical theater.

JONATHAN PITTS is the executive producer and cofounder of the Chicago Improv Festival, and recently *New City Magazine* included him in their annual "Top 50

Players of Chicago Theater" list. He's also been an improv instructor for The Second City Training Center for the past five years.

DAVID RAZOWSKY, artistic director of The Second City Los Angeles, has written and performed in ten Second City Chicago revues and has directed The Second City Los Angeles, The Second City Detroit, and the National Touring Company. David is an alumnus of ImprovOlympic, a cofounder of the Annoyance Theater, and a member of The Reduced Shakespeare Company. He's directed two of Amsterdam's Boom Chicago productions. David is the voice of Dixon in ABC's animated series *The Weekenders* and has appeared on *Spin City, Roseanne, Working,* and *Late Night with David Letterman* as the voice of Albert Brooks's parrot.

BERNIE SAHLINS is one of the cofounders of The Second City; during his tenure he produced and directed sixty-five shows. Bernie continues producing and directing in Chicago, including a show for Chicago's Museum of Science and Industry, and has also published translations of several plays.

AVERY SCHREIBER, a Chicago native and Goodman School of Drama graduate, studied with the legendary Viola Spolin at the request of her son, Paul Sills, and later joined the famed Second City improv group in 1960. It was there Avery met his lifelong friend, Jack Burns, and together they formed the unforgettable comic duo Burns and Schreiber. After his run with Second City, Avery worked with the Committee in San Francisco, as both a performer and a director. He then joined Paul Sills's Story Theater production of Ovid's *Metamorphoses* in Los Angeles and on Broadway, for which he won the Los Angeles Drama Critics Circle Award for Best Actor. Avery was an accomplished actor and dedicated improv coach. He taught for more than thirty-five years to thousands of students who attended his workshops all over the country.

BRIAN STACK, after studying at The Second City Training Center and ImprovOlympic, toured with The Second City National Touring Company for two years. He then joined The Second City ETC cast, cocreating three revues before moving to New York in 1997 to work as a writer/performer on *Late Night with Conan O'Brien,* where he continues to work today. He is married to fellow Second City alum Miriam Tolan and has two children.

RON WEST has worked for The Second City on and off since 1982, when he appeared in *The Life and Adventures of Nicholas Nickleby,* an 8½ production. He performed in and directed a lot of shows at The Second City, the last of which was *Curious George Goes to War.* Those two shows are the bookends, so ask Ron for details about other fun times where he was very blessed to work with talented people. He's friends with most of them, which is more important, anyway. He lives in Los Angeles where he recently cowrote and directed *The Andrea and Hep Show,* which was a blast.

FRED WILLARD joined The Second City Chicago in 1965. After Second City, Fred joined the Ace Trucking Company improv comedy group, played the lead in Alan Arkin's production of *Little Murders* off-Broadway, and then went on to do many commercials and a lot of TV and films including *This Is Spinal Tap, First Family, Waiting for Guffman, Best in Show,* and *Austin Powers: The Spy Who Shagged Me.*

ABOUT THE AUTHOR

ANNE LIBERA is the artistic director of The Second City Training Center and a resident director for The Second City. Her directing credits include The Second City productions of *The Madness of Curious George* and *Computer Chips and Salsa,* and Second City National Touring Company productions seen all over the United States as well as productions in Vienna, Austria, and Edinburgh, Scotland. Anne is on the faculty at Columbia College Chicago, and serves as an artistic consultant to the Museum of Science and Industry. A graduate of Northwestern University, Anne reviewed theater on WGN radio and contributed to the NPR news quiz show *Wait, Wait . . . Don't Tell Me!* Anne serves on the governing board for Gilda's Club Chicago and lives in Chicago with her husband, Kelly Leonard, and her children, Nicholas and Eleanor.